Praise

CW00502698

'The concept of a Personal Board was alien to me. However, it has now become apparent that it could play a critical role in achieving my career vision, especially now that I am pursuing a portfolio career.'
— **Tribeni Chougule**, Diversity Leader

'It's a really interesting and innovative concept that I wish I had discovered years ago. As a founder, I've already started implementing some of Emma's suggestions and I can see how powerful it's going to be for both the business's growth... and my own! Highly recommended.'
— **Laura Harnett**, Founder, Seep

'Five stars! I hadn't heard of the Personal Board concept before and, being new to entrepreneurship, I am now using this concept to build my support network and customer base.'
— **Jules White**, Founder, Creativa

'A must-read for new-founders and entrepreneurs everywhere. A structured approach to thinking about how to activate your network to achieve your goals faster.'
— **Lucy Rhodes**, Angel Investor

'Successful careers are built with flourishing networks. An inspirational book with insights that I wish I'd systematically applied throughout my career.'
— **Laura Turner**, Sales Professional

'Sage advice, delivered in a structured and methodical way. For both the young and tenured professionals who want to create opportunity through their network.'
— **Genevieve Martin**, Senior Tech Leader

EMMA MASLEN

THE PERSONAL BOARD OF YOU INC.

How to recruit the best personal
advisors to accelerate achievement

R^ethink

First published in Great Britain in 2023
by Rethink Press (www.rethinkpress.com)

© Copyright Emma Maslen

All rights reserved. No part of this publication may be reproduced, stored in or introduced into a retrieval system, or transmitted, in any form, or by any means (electronic, mechanical, photocopying, recording or otherwise) without the prior written permission of the publisher.

The right of Emma Maslen to be identified as the author of this work has been asserted by her in accordance with the Copyright, Designs and Patents Act 1988.

This book is sold subject to the condition that it shall not, by way of trade or otherwise, be lent, resold, hired out, or otherwise circulated without the publisher's prior consent in any form of binding or cover other than that in which it is published and without a similar condition including this condition being imposed on the subsequent purchaser.

Cover image © Shutterstock | Roman Samborskyi

For Doug, who provided the pen.

For Tribeni and Matt, who inspired the finish.

For Martin, Tom and Ben, for indulging me. Always.

Contents

Introduction

Over the years, despite holding down a full-time job, I have also adopted the role of part-time career advisor. This was never part of my plan, and yet it has become the most rewarding part of my career to date.

I frequently receive calls from people looking for advice on the next step of their career journey. Some of these people I know well, but others I have met only once. Indeed, only yesterday, before writing this introduction, I took three calls from people asking for help with their careers.

Why do people call me? Ten years ago, I wouldn't have had an answer.

People need support from those who are open to listening, working through problems and helping others find their way, make the path clearer and easier to navigate and, most importantly, easier to achieve. I have been lucky enough always to have known people who are happy to help me in both my personal life and my working career. When you are navigating your journey through life, the impact others can make should never be underestimated.

I'll share some of my own stories in this book as well as those of other people I've met. These stories serve to illustrate some of the amazing gifts others can bestow on your career.

Why am I writing this book? Why do I want to help? The answers to those questions are simple. I have been both the receiver and the provider of help. While I am grateful for every leg-up I have been given, I get an enormous boost from being the person who helps too. I also feel fulfilled when I see people accomplishing what they have set out to achieve and reaching the goals they have set for themselves.

However, while I will take a call from anybody, there's only one of me and so many hours in the day, and I realised I would be able to help *more* people by writing this book. In it, you will find the staple advice I have given over the years, which also helps others recognise what is possible.

I would love people to be inspired – for them to read one of the stories in this book and think, 'That's just how I was', 'That's exactly what happened to me', or 'That's just what I was going through at the time', giving them the confidence to break away, to try something different and to take action.

This book is for anybody – regardless of age or demographics – who wants to build a better future for themselves and take ownership of their development, their career and their life's goals. From an existing CEO to a wannabe yoga studio owner, everyone will find something in this book to further their goals.

My Personal Board revelation

Thirteen years ago, I reached a crossroads in my career. I was working for Sun Microsystems, a large technology business which was being acquired by another technology giant, Oracle. During the acquisition period, I was offered two new roles – one internally and one externally – and found myself sweating over my next move. I deliberated at length, painstakingly weighing up the pros and cons of leaving a company and a job I loved versus moving to a new, unknown role that would deliver better career acceleration.

As I considered my options, I started to receive a lot of advice from those around me. Over a few evenings, my husband and I sat at the kitchen table while

I offloaded the latest opinion I had received. However, we found we weren't getting anywhere. I was frustrated, as every recommendation I heard didn't sit right with me. I felt the advice was based on other people's experiences rather than my unique situation and perspective.

Then I experienced a sudden revelation. Not of the hallelujah type, but a rare sense of overwhelming clarity. Every person who had offered me advice had been one of my peers at Sun Microsystems. I had not sought outside opinions, except from my husband. I hadn't even asked my previous mentors for guidance, despite them having been fantastic in helping me steer my career to that point.

My revelation was this: What if I thought of myself as a company, Emma Maslen Inc., rather than as a person? Assuming I was CEO of this company, how would I structure any new advice and guidance? I pictured a company board advising a CEO and then imagined a diverse group of experienced people sitting around my kitchen table, holding the first Emma Maslen Inc. board meeting. My own Personal Board.

Who should be sitting at the table? What would they tell me? How would they help me to mitigate any risk? Considering how outside perspectives would help, I realised I needed objective and diverse opinions… and fast. I scribbled down a list of people

I would call in the morning and held a virtual board meeting in my head. Then I sounded out my new Personal Board's views and opinions.

Ever since, I have been developing and refining the concept of a Personal Board. Over the years, it has helped me to achieve my goals faster, mitigate the risks when undertaking significant career transitions, and find more joy in my work.

That is the essence of this book. Having developed the process for myself, I have seen how it can significantly expand career horizons, delivering more opportunities, more choices and more clarity on the right road. Often, at events or when I am mentoring, people ask me for my best piece of career advice. I *always* start with my Personal Board concept.

It's amazing how many tenured professionals forget to think strategically about the people they engage with in their careers. Their approach is ineffective for two reasons:

1. By not thinking strategically about your connections, you only use your organic connections – those you have unintentionally collected, including friends, family and colleagues – to make progress. Typically, these are the same people you have always relied on – the people in your immediate network. If there is no diversity, how can you maximise progress?

2. We all hope that life is a meritocracy, with rewards based on what we know rather than who we know. However, if you are not strategically extending your network, and you remain unknown to the people making decisions about big opportunities, how will those people recognise your merits? Also, if you don't tell people what you are looking for next, how can they think of you when the right opportunity arises?

Whether you are just starting your first job, are undergoing a career transition, or are an established senior executive or an entrepreneur embarking on a new journey, this book will give you a new perspective – one that will help you to progress in life. You'll find ideas on how to expand your network, develop your brand and push yourself to new heights, and even how to use your network when things get tough.

This book includes practical advice gathered both from my personal experience and from others who have created Personal Boards. Armed with this knowledge, you too can build, develop and operate your own Personal Board, which will accelerate you towards your goals.

How to use this book

This book aims to encourage you to take control of your career, your connections and the advice and help you seek. You may choose to read it from cover to cover in one sitting, but if – like me – you prefer to work your way through a book in bite-sized chunks, it is structured accordingly, complete with highlighted sections. These include:

- **Personal stories:** We often learn best from others' successes and failures. The real-life case studies I have included might be the easiest way for you to remember what works best and what you should avoid.

- **Practical tips:** These are my actionable tips on what's worked best for me; for example, how to use social media to expand your network, or how to set goals.

- **Background information:** Inspiration for some of my concepts originates from research or analogies. These points are included to illustrate those concepts and to spark your imagination.

The first part of this book (Chapters 1–4) deals with my ideas and theories behind setting up a Personal Board, such as the elements behind a successful corporate board.

The second part (Chapters 5–7) deals with the practicalities of creating a Personal Board.

The third part (Chapters 8–10) deals with practical scenarios, including how to use your Personal

Board to secure a new job or promotion or to set up a new business.

Finally, Chapter 11 gives a short recap and further motivation for you to start your own Personal Board journey.

In a nutshell: This book will tell you how to create an imaginary concept; fill it with real people, experiences and advice; and use it as an active career management tool to make things happen. Let's get started on creating your Personal Board.

1
Personal Boards: What's The Big Idea?

In this first chapter, I will illustrate the basic principles of my Personal Board concept, giving you a clear understanding of how it looks, feels and works. I'll also introduce you to one of the fundamental principles of the Personal Board: the importance of reaching further out for fresh advice and new perspectives.

What your Personal Board might look like

There is an old saying that the people with the best advice are usually the ones who have been through the most.

One of the areas I receive the most questions about is the form and forum of the Personal Board.

Imagine you have the services of a corporate board at your disposal – your own Personal Board – the best and brightest minds in business to help you progress your hopes, your dreams and your career. Don't worry if you don't have experience of how a corporate board works – I will talk about that point in Chapter 3.

I have a vision of my Personal Board, starting with the boardroom. I imagine a large, beautifully decorated room – perhaps a corner office overlooking Central Park – with modern decor, a glass table, white chairs and mood lighting. High-quality teas and coffees are steaming away on a side table... My scene is set.

I am sitting at the boardroom table, waiting for my Personal Board members to walk through the door to start my meeting. They're a mix of respected mentors, coaches, colleagues and friends.

When I think about my current Personal Board, I consider myself blessed to have such a diverse group of individuals seated around my boardroom table:

- Personal connections
  - My husband
  - Three school friends
    - A small-business coach
    - A marketeer
    - An engineer (of helicopters, no less)

- Industry connections
  - The chairman of a FTSE 250 company
  - The CEO of a US company
  - A career salesperson
  - A serial entrepreneur

- Development connections
  - A C-suite executive coach
  - A founder of an investment firm

Each of these board members can provide guidance, advice or a different perspective on the issues that regularly confront me. Some are senior to me, some are junior and some are working in parallel industries. Some, such as my husband, are not in the industry at all. Some knew they had been invited to sit on my Personal Board, while others are people I go to for ad hoc advice and guidance whenever I need it.

Once my Personal Board members have arrived, I will tell them about my goals, my achievements to date, my next steps and my plans for the future, plotting my journey forward.

A regular meeting of minds

The Personal Board concept is a virtual one. I have described a boardroom setting, but that is an imaginary concept. It helps me to visualise my set of advisors in a formal but welcoming setting, but in practice, I approach each person individually. They are a series of people I talk to separately whenever I need help in deciding where I should go next and what actions I need to take.

Ideally, I meet these people face to face, but sometimes we chat on the phone. Occasionally, I might meet two people together in person to discuss a certain subject, but it's never with all of my Personal Board together 'boardroom-style'.

In short: The concept is about having a regular group of people who can share, coach and help you with your goals, typically on a one-to-one basis. It's important to note that people should give their advice free of charge, and they should always have your best interests at heart. This might at first make you think it safer to turn to the people closest to you, but there are lots of benefits to reaching out to others.

Organic conversations versus strategising to find the right people

If you want to hear how good you are, you can simply listen to your friends. If you want to hear how good you *could* be, you need to listen to a wider circle of people – those who can offer you dispassionate advice. This is one of the fundamental principles of a Personal Board.

We all have conversations with people we have organically 'collected' along our journey. Let's take a moment to celebrate those conversations and relationships. I certainly know I wouldn't be successful today without them.

MY STORY: Early influences

The original devil and angel on my shoulder

Throughout my life, I've always had two voices simultaneously talking to me – one spurring me on and the other forcing me to doubt myself. I put it down to my formative years at school and two teachers in particular: Mr Williams and Mr Manley.

I have working-class parents, who did everything they could for the family. My mum worked full-time as a head cook at a retirement home. My dad was made redundant after seventeen years at the Lipton Tea factory, where he'd often worked double shifts due to economic necessity.

Having achieved my GCSEs, I was studying three Science A levels, as I intended to go on to train as a doctor. However, after my dad was made redundant, I realised there wasn't any hope of me being able to fund medical school, especially as I didn't want to put any further financial pressure on my parents.

Handing my books back to my science teacher, Mr Williams, was tough. 'You will amount to nothing without an education,' he told me sternly.

It was with trepidation that I approached my maths teacher, Mr Manley. He was kindness personified: 'Choose your path. If it doesn't work out, you can always come back.'

I've had these devil- and angel-type creatures on my shoulders ever since. These two voices have shaped my work ethic and my constant need to keep pushing myself.

One says: Further your education. Keep developing.

The other says: Try something else. Worst-case scenario, you can always go back.

Great advice for anyone!

You can gain great advice from unsolicited and organic sources. Personal Boards can be made up of organic connections and targeted connections, and some members stay with you for life.

Organic relationships can be great in providing advice and encouragement. However, if your aim is to accelerate your achievement, why wouldn't you stop and think about how you could *improve* that advice?

One of the reasons I developed the idea of a Personal Board for working through my situations was that the advice I had been receiving fell into the same categories every time:

- **Predictable:** Lacking diversity; from the same contacts, peers and friends

- **Filtered:** Where I sometimes didn't get the whole opinion

- **Biased:** Where the advice was often based on their own situations and experiences

- **Unwanted source:** Where, especially in the early days, advice was given freely by many people

Having realised I was not refreshing the sources of my advice, I started to think about how I could take on different views and perspectives. I then took that a step further and thought, 'If I could approach *anyone* for advice, who should I choose?'

It helps to supplement your board with new, diverse sources. This is the biggest difference in selecting your advisors strategically rather than only gathering them organically. Your Personal Board needs to evolve as your career progresses. I still have Personal Board members who have been with me since school, but I have added new members, depending on my changing development plans and my progress concerning my goals.

ANTHEA'S STORY: Aim high

Punch above your weight

Anthea, an entrepreneur in the FinTech space, gives us a great example of how to strategise on who you take advice from.

I started working with Anthea in 2017, when she and her husband, Sam, were setting up their business. Finance was one of the key areas they were developing technology for.

We were having a chat one day about the Personal Board idea, which allows entrepreneurs to plug knowledge gaps quickly to help them grow. We discussed who was currently giving Anthea and Sam advice. They were receiving unvarying guidance and, on reflection, the advisors were also similar – limited diversity in background and therefore limited diversity o opinion.

We started to consider the question 'If you could have anyone advising you, who would it be?'

Trying to think laterally, we discussed:

- Backgrounds and experience
- Customer connections
- Potential funding connections

We went from discussing expensive but low-level advisors to contemplating approaching some of the most senior people in the finance and banking industry.

We brainstormed using some of the techniques in this book and quickly came up with criteria, plus a list of names for Anthea to approach. The results were amazing.

Within six weeks, Anthea and Sam had two senior advisors – from HSBC and Credit Suisse – advising their business.

Reflecting with Anthea months later, breaking out of her network and considering the 'art of the possible' for formulating her Personal Board made a substantial difference to the speed at which she and her husband were able to grow their business.

Organic connections can be great, but why not aim higher and wider to get a greater breadth of connections and support for you and your goals?

Chapter review

This chapter has laid the foundations for your Personal Board by examining the elements of successful corporate boards.

Key takeaways

- A Personal Board is a concept – no tea and coffee required. The idea is to conceptualise a meeting of experienced minds rather than arranging physical meetings. You're looking for frequent contact with your board members.

- Organic is good, but purposeful wins the day. Organic relationships and advice are always helpful. However, think about the opinions and help you are missing out on if you fail to strategically seek out different or higher-level views beyond your immediate circle.

• A Personal Board comprises your best advisors at any stage of your career. Think of this as a way for you to strategically consider the advice you are seeking and accumulate the help you need to accelerate your achievements.

EXERCISE: Picture your board

Take a moment to visualise your Personal Board, and then consider:

• Who is at your table today?

• How are they helping you to achieve your life's ambitions?

• What might you be missing?

2
How, When And
Where This Works

When is the best time to set up a Personal Board? The answer, as the adage goes: There's no time like the present. If you're already thinking about it, it's time to start the process.

A common mistake is to think that Personal Boards are only suitable for high flyers in the prime of their careers in high-tech industries. You may well think a Personal Board isn't relevant to you, for example, because you're not a certain type of person, or not that ambitious or not in a particular industry.

The principles behind the Personal Board can be applied all the way through your career and for different types of roles, including:

- Junior role
- First job
- Mid-career post
- Entrepreneurial employment
- Part-time work
- Executive position
- Non-executive directorship

The Personal Board is such a flexible concept that it can be adapted to practically any person and any situation. You only need to have the confidence to embrace it.

Is a Personal Board relevant to me?

There are lots of reasons you might be thinking that a Personal Board isn't right for you, for example:

- 'I'm not important enough to need one.'
- 'It's easier for people higher up to make those senior connections, right?'
- 'This isn't for junior people, is it?'
- 'I'm already successful so don't need the help.'

I have found many applications and successes in using a Personal Board at *all* levels, although there are slightly different applications. In this section, I will talk through the typical stages of people's careers and give some ideas about the benefits of a Personal Board at each stage.

Starting a new career

Having a Personal Board doesn't mean that you already have a fully formed plan and career roadmap in mind. It can be something much smaller in scale – think of it as a starter pack for your career path.

Perhaps you have just left school or will soon be finishing college or university, and you need to decide what to do and where to go next. Or maybe you are thinking about your own child at the outset of their career. The obvious people to turn to initially for advice are those who know you or your child best, including:

- Parents and carers
- Other relatives
- Siblings
- Friends
- Teachers

I'm sure all those people will give great advice, but remember that it will be organic advice, coming from the same people that have always spoken to you or your child.

Think now about who else you have access to in your network. Can you think of someone who doesn't know you or your child's situation intimately, and who might be able to give more objective and practical advice than those listed above? Or, frankly, who could offer a better opportunity?

BETH'S STORY: A junior personal board

Legal eagle

I was catching up with Lyn, a friend of mine, over a coffee. She mentioned her daughter, Beth, who is super-bright and ambitious and was midway through her law degree. Beth was thinking about her graduate placement and what she might do after university... but had hit a stumbling block.

Beth was applying for the same roles as thousands of other students. As an anonymous candidate, she was struggling to get a break for a placement. I suggested Beth should join me at an upcoming networking event sponsored by Penningtons Manches Cooper, a large law firm based in London. Beth came along to the event and, after a couple of quick conversations, I was able to introduce her to the CEO of Penningtons.

Beth picked up some great tips and tricks from the CEO, which she later put into practice – not only for landing her graduate placement but also, subsequently, for securing a permanent role after leaving university.

A Personal Board can help make those valuable early connections to get you started on your journey.

Mid-career: Promotions and progressions

There is a broad range of mid-career applications for a Personal Board. If you have held several roles and are considering the next part of your journey, a Personal Board will actively help drive your career progression in many ways.

Development plans and direction

First, Personal Boards can help formulate that all-important development plan. Often, it's when we are mid-career – fairly established – that we want to take hold of our career and consider how we can achieve our goals and objectives. However, if we don't solicit diverse opinions and independent advice, we may commit ourselves 'blind' to an opportunity.

Using a Personal Board will help you explore possibilities before you nail yourself to the mast. While you are busy building your career plan, it's almost impossible to appreciate *all* the possibilities available. Seeking advice and guidance from others, with a broad range of experience, will help you to expand your options.

Building your brand and your reputation

Once you have established yourself in an industry or embarked on a certain career path, you might consider yourself to have already arrived at your destination. However, along the way, you may have missed out on opportunities by failing to take feedback onboard.

A well-rounded group of individuals, who can provide feedback on your reputation, your development areas and any future actions you might need to take, will be invaluable knowledge to accelerate your achievement.

It is not uncommon to push for promotion or progress without first seeking any feedback, perhaps because we are fearful of what we may receive in return. Whether you are fearful or not, it's crazy not to gather as much information as possible before you embark on a campaign. Why *wouldn't* you use a trusted group of people you respect to help guide your plans? It will inevitably result in a greater chance of success.

Validating your brand and reputation is an easy win with a Personal Board.

Stakeholder management

It's a fact of life: If you are unknown to the people making the key decisions about a role or opportunity, they will not think of you.

Personal Board members can help in many ways with stakeholder management. In the first instance, they can support the simple task of mapping out the key stakeholders:

- Who will influence the decision on an opportunity?

- Do you know them and what do you know about them?

- Do they know you?

- What do they know about you?

We want life to be a meritocracy and for people to notice us, but the world is a noisy place. If you don't promote yourself and manage people's views of you, then you are leaving them to filter the noise, simply hoping they conclude you are the best person for the job.

Strategising about who makes decisions regarding your future has considerable value. Second, it's likely that the people you are asking for advice could also, in the future, themselves be influencers or even stakeholders. If you have cleverly assembled the right board members and shared your goals and aspirations with them, you will have chosen at least a couple of people who can have some influence on achieving those goals.

Senior career

Even if you are already established in your chosen industry, everything I have said above about first-career and mid-career uses for a Personal Board is also applicable to senior positions. With that in mind, ensure that you read the details on all the other career stages, which will also give you inspiration for your Personal Board.

NIALL'S STORY: Preparing for a promotion

Taking the next step

Niall was in his early forties and ready to take the next step into sales management. He had been working for his existing company for three years and had created a reputation fit for the foundations of promotion. However, the macroeconomic climate wasn't helping his progress.

Even though his first-line manager had confirmed Niall stood a great chance of success in the next promotion, everything had slowed down under COVID, including the role that Niall would be applying for.

Niall and I met to talk about his strategy for getting the role.

While the macroeconomic climate hadn't been helping the situation, our discussion revealed that the only person Niall had spoken to about taking that next step was his immediate (first-line) manager. He hadn't consulted his second-line manager, directors, peers or key stakeholders.

When I delved a little deeper into who the stakeholders were, three things became clear:

1. We didn't know their criteria for the hiring decision.
2. We didn't know who they would be sponsoring for the role.
3. We didn't know a) if they were aware Niall wanted the role or b) if they thought he met the criteria.

We quickly hatched a plan.

Niall mapped out all the key stakeholders and then arranged to meet with them. We sketched out some questions before the meetings so we could understand their criteria and ensure that Niall's persona and reputation reflected that he was the prime candidate for the role.

At the time of meeting, it was three months until the end of the financial year. This gave us some time, as most organisations release new headcount numbers at the beginning of the financial year.

Niall and I agreed to meet every couple of weeks to check in on his progress.

The result? Niall was offered the position in January, to start in February.

A Personal Board can help you plan for a promotion or your next move by playing devil's advocate, revealing potential obstacles and helping you overcome them.

Reverse mentoring

The world is a fast-moving place. We need to adapt to the changes. When I started we were not blessed with platforms like LinkedIn to find the right connections in a split second.

Many industries are being disrupted by radically different ways of thinking. Airbnb, Uber and Fiverr are just three examples of companies that have found fresh ways of doing business. As a senior executive, how do you ensure you remain up to date with new ideas and thinking? How do you understand where the market is going? How do you stay current and foster innovation?

Reverse mentoring is a perfect solution to these challenges. Reverse mentoring is about junior employees, in a variety of roles, mentoring people senior to them. Carefully selected matches between senior and junior mentors inject new ideas into the business, helping the mentees get a finger on the pulse of change.

From full-time to portfolio

One of the best uses for a Personal Board is when an experienced individual is looking to move away from their full-time career and consider something more freelance, consultative, part-time or portfolio.

Everybody's networks include people who have:

- Set up their own business as a consultant
- Moved from a full-time to a part-time role
- Changed from one employer to many, ie, adopted a portfolio career

These major career changes give a perfect example of how to maximise the benefits of a Personal Board. Often, we may need months to lay the foundations: creating a business plan, identifying potential customers, considering finance options, consulting with lawyers and accountants, etc.

You can shortcut this process by talking to people who are experienced in your situation. This will allow you to assess an opportunity more quickly and ensure you haven't missed anything in the transition. Adding two to three new people to your Personal Board who have relevant knowledge will also help crystallise your vision, fuel your passion for the opportunity and help you de-risk any move by knowing the pitfalls in advance.

Moving into self-employment or a portfolio career, or becoming an entrepreneur, can be a lonely place at first. It is often overlooked that, on becoming a consultant, you will lose your immediate peer group – the people you find around you in any reasonably sized organisation, including your teammates, customers and partners. Within organisations, these groups are already established and continue to grow organically. When you branch out alone, your Personal Board will allow you to create new peer groups and keep your support network intact.

MY STORY: Building a portfolio

Finding a new peer group

After I had been angel investing for a couple of years, I found myself inexorably drawn to the start-up world.

Large corporations had been a haven for me throughout my working life. However, the start-up world offered a fast-moving pace and a fresh outlook, where my corporate experience could result in quick wins.

Almost all of the start-ups I've had the pleasure of dealing with have had vibrant, magnetic founders at the helm – salespeople excellent for both their vision and their business. With this in mind, I decided I'd like to work with more start-ups going forward.,

However, it wasn't obvious how my everyday peer group could help me in this new world. Most had committed themselves to the corporate ladder and didn't have networks with the smaller-business world in place. I therefore decided to reach out to my network to see who I could recruit for the right advice and support.

I brainstormed to identify:

1. **Same journey – Established**

   Someone who had followed the same path as me and was now established in that world or role

2. **Same journey – Early days**

   Someone on the same journey who had made the leap but wasn't yet fully established

3. **Start-ups – Expert**

   Someone who already knew what I was trying to find out, who could help with my journey and connections

Having always worked hard to keep growing my network, I quickly identified three people who could potentially help me. All were able to offer me invaluable support and guidance, in both how to initially break into the start-up world and how to prosper once I had done so.

Personal Board members can be of all backgrounds and often have walked the same path, just before you. Why not benefit from their learning and hindsight?

Practical uses for a Personal Board

You may already have some ideas on how people have helped you throughout your career but still wonder when and why you would need a Personal Board in the future. If you are going to accumulate some of the best minds in the world to help you achieve your goals, you might be thinking, 'What can I use them for?' and, 'What is the benefit of calling on this group of people for regular input and advice into my goals and career?'

The following is a list – by no means exhaustive – of how I have seen others benefit from Personal Boards.

Finding a new role

At any stage of our lives, the goals and achievements we strive to achieve are influenced by others. Whether it's the people we would like to work for, or the customers we would like to work with, our goals are to some extent in other people's hands.

When I was starting in my career, we talked about six degrees of separation, meaning everyone in the world could be reached in six relationship hops. For example, you know one person, who knows someone else, who knows another person, who knows someone, who knows someone else... who can finally, by association, connect you to Elton John.

Now that we have larger professional networks and multiple social media platforms, it is estimated you can reach anyone in the world in only three or four hops. That makes our networks more powerful, with other people easier to reach than ever before. In these networks, you will find people who can accelerate your success and achievement.

ABBY'S STORY: Reach out to your network

The power of connections

At the beginning of 2020, having graduated and joined a graduate management scheme with a well-respected car rental company, Abby decided she wanted to advance her career.

In July 2020, during the pandemic, Abby made the hardest decision of her life to date, taking voluntary redundancy in pursuit of career advancement.

Abby recalled a speaker at a leadership conference saying, 'You never want to sit in the comfortable seat'.

Opting for redundancy was a brave step. However, as Abby left her role, the world shifted to adjust to the COVID pandemic, and Abby's path ahead was by no means clear.

I knew Abby's brother, Tom, from my years in the IT industry. Abby and I had met before her redundancy at one of my Personal Board events, and I remember at the time being highly impressed by her. When I heard Abby was between roles and struggling in her search, I reached out to see if I could help.

We spent some time together brainstorming ideas, which helped her incorporate a business approach into her career planning and development, while also creating her own Personal Board.

Armed with a few ideas and low-touch connections, Abby expanded her network to multiple companies, increasing her knowledge in events, working with mentors from Plan B Mentoring (now called Balance the Board), and making connections that would ultimately lead to a new role.

Abby identified a mentor, who she still meets every month. She has found this invaluable – having somebody providing impartial, sound and honest advice.

By her own admission, the extra connections and events helped Abby's confidence skyrocket and opened many more doors. She realises that continuing to invest in herself, enrolling on courses and developing herself further, have all been possible due to advice from her connections.

Abby's network and the support and guidance she received, along with the advice on interviewing techniques and preparation, resulted in her securing three job opportunities within three different industries in the space of six weeks.

Since then, Abby has achieved a promotion, from a team manager role to department manager. She now oversees 150 colleagues and the whole operation of her new company.

Personal Boards can connect you to known and unknown opportunities. You only need to invest a little time in your network to reveal the possibilities.

Gaining knowledge for advancement

When you take on new roles, move companies or start a new business, there is often a knowledge gap. Put frankly, there should be. You need to push yourself beyond your comfort zones, so you shouldn't expect to have all the knowledge in place – first, to get a new role, and second, to be successful in it.

Perhaps you are looking for a new role, but you haven't quite worked out how to gain the right experience or connections to make that next step. Often the missing answers lie in your existing network. This presents a prime example of the benefits of using a Personal Board: not just in securing your next role but also in helping you prepare for the new position.

MY STORY: Reconnecting with Peter

One connection away

When I turned forty, I reflected on my career over the previous twenty years and considered what the next twenty might hold.

One of my key objectives was to join a board and start to acquire some non-executive director experience. My motivation for this was to build towards a portfolio career in the future, working with multiple companies.

A traditional road for me would have been to buy every book under the sun and look for the answers in the text. However, by now well-practised at using my network for input, I decided there was probably a faster route.

I sat down and asked myself, 'Who do I know on a board?' After twenty minutes of racking my brain and trying to think of someone, I remembered my connection with Peter.

I had worked for him at Sun Microsystems when he was senior vice president of worldwide sales. Peter had had an amazing career, both before and after Sun, and it struck me that he had recently become the chairman of a FTSE-listed company.

To clarify: I had met Peter only three or four times. Fortunately, one occasion was on an Achievers Club trip, so I was sure he'd at least vaguely know who I was.

Opening LinkedIn, I took a punt...

Hey Peter,

Not sure if you remember me, but I was wondering if I could trouble you for a piece of advice? I'm really interested in getting onto a board. Could you share your story with me – how you went from executive to chairman of the board? Could you give me some tips on the steps you took to get there?

I didn't think he'd reply to my LinkedIn message, though this says more about my imposter syndrome than about Peter's demeanour. Within half an hour, he replied and dropped me his mobile number, along with some good times to chat.

Peter gave me forty-five minutes, during which he shared some real gems of advice, which I've noted below for those interested in joining a board one day:

1. The leap from executive to the board is hard... for anyone. Your job is to convince people about what you can do, rather than what you have done.
2. Education and accreditations are key. Get an Institute of Directors qualification.
3. Network with boards. The first board is all about who you know. Talk to people. Share your interests.

Three years on, I had ticked every box and achieved my goal.

Could I have made that progress without the call to Peter? Sure, but the road would have been significantly longer, as I would have needed to plot the path myself.

Our networks are full of people who have walked the path before us, most of whom thrive on sharing their experiences to help others. Add them to your own board to get regular advice and progression.

Starting somewhere new

Life moves fast, and things will often happen before you have had time to properly plan your journey. Your Personal Board will help you in settling in and broadening your network after you have moved to a new role, company, industry or country.

KIM'S STORY: International networking

How to fit in fast

Kim moved to London from the USA, in late 2019, to work in a European role. While she knew her new role involved travel, Kim expected to spend most of her time in London, so she was keen to make connections and get used to living in the UK.

Settling into a new country can be easier if you have family connections and kids in school. From my own experiences of living abroad without kids or family, I know it's important to invest in connections quickly.

I met Kim through a mutual former employer, who had suggested that, as women in tech leadership, we would share some common ground and be able to support each other.

On talking with Kim, it became clear she had an entrepreneurial spirit and a real passion for STEM (science, technology, engineering, medicine). She was established in the tech business, and she also enjoyed mentoring and working with earlier-stage businesses.

An initial connection from me to an angel investing community quickly fed Kim's passion for the entrepreneurial world and expanded her network into the London market.

As the pandemic hit, and visions of brunching and sightseeing in London soon evaporated, this angel investment community became the backbone of Kim's support network during the lonely lockdown months. Kim made long-term friends and connections in that community as well as feeding her passion for getting more women and girls into STEM subjects.

Personal Boards are useful in expanding your current contacts.

Setting up a new business

Personal Boards are not only about corporate careers. Entrepreneurs in any industry benefit from setting up an entrepreneurial Personal Board.

I will cover the differences between a Personal Board and a real-life corporate board later on since entrepreneurs embarking on a start-up journey are likely to have both.

For this example: Entrepreneurs need to be thinking about how they can use and expand their network to quickly scale their business. The personal network is often invaluable in the early days of a business when cash is tight and you'll need a favour or two. *All* entrepreneurs will also have personal areas in need of development – for example, their skills in running a business, the sales skills required to sell the product or company, or the industry knowledge needed for operating in a new space.

LEE AND CHRIS'S STORY: Building an entrepreneurial Personal Board

From apprentice to SaaS (software as a service) mastermind

Entrepreneurs Lee and Chris were in the process of building a software company. Both were young, engaging and enthusiastic. Indeed, Lee had won the BBC's *The Apprentice* ten years prior so was used to dealing with pressure and publicity.

Lee and Chris's business was originally a services business; however, their customers had driven demand for the creation of a software platform in which people saw the value and wanted to buy. Almost overnight, it went from a services business, in which they had lots of experience, to a SaaS/tech business, in which they had no experience whatsoever.

Using their networks, Lee and Chris started to reach out to people they knew who might be able to help them. It was at that point that Chris and I had a chance meeting through a mutual friend.

I got together with both Chris and Lee, and we talked about how they could transform into a SaaS business. In talking this through, we established there were four areas where they required additional support:

1. Technology roadmap
2. Software contracts and pricing

3. Start-up fundraising
4. Partnerships and alliances

In an hour of brainstorming, we came up with five people in the industry that Chris and Lee could connect with, to start gathering knowledge and support and to help them develop their idea into a thriving business.

With a core group of advisors quickly established, Lee and Chris launched their new business within nine months. They are now on a great growth trajectory.

An interesting aside to this story is that Lee and Chris were approached by several consultants, who wanted to provide similar help and information at a considerable cost. The advisors we found were mostly pro bono at the early stages of getting the business up and running.

Personal Boards can expand your network, plugging knowledge gaps and providing new opportunities.

Career transition or building a portfolio career

I am only in my forties, but I have already had several careers: as a salesperson, leader, consultant, property owner and – now – an author.

According to Dawn Rosenberg McKay, the average person will have five or six careers in their lifetime. It's therefore likely you will change jobs more than once, each time needing new skills, new connections and more help.

Portfolio careers (careers including multiple positions at one time) and the gig economy (chiefly contract and temporary work) have become increasingly popular. They have been accelerated by The Great Resignation – the higher-than-usual number of employees voluntarily leaving their jobs since late 2020. However, frequently changing jobs requires planning and a different way of thinking.

JULES'S STORY: Career change from employment to entrepreneur

All change in a pandemic

Jules worked in a hair and beauty salon for most of her working life. While in the beauty industry, Jules had always been quite techy and interested to explore the online world.

During the COVID lockdowns, when the salon was closed, Jules realised the pandemic was the catalyst she needed to change her career, from being employed in a salon to becoming an entrepreneur and starting her own business.

In the ideation stage, Jules asked some close friends for some connections to start exploring freelance roles in marketing. Through one of her friends, she connected with Michelle, a personal assistant.

Michelle's business helps lots of small businesses with marketing and administration services. She and Jules discussed how websites could provide the creative outlet and challenge that Jules had been looking for. She was introduced to the world of WordPress and started her journey to become an expert in building websites. Using her interest in WordPress as an anchor, Jules then joined several networking groups and began building her network of similarly-minded individuals and entrepreneurs who had walked the path before her.

As the pandemic ended, Jules launched her own business, supported by her new skillset and network.

Personal Boards provide essential advice, skills and new networks.

Clearing blind spots

One of the biggest and most useful objectives for having a Personal Board is to gain feedback for improvement. This case is useful for anyone – young, old, new, tenured, corporate or entrepreneurial.

Structured feedback from different perspectives provides new insight into your strengths and weaknesses, which you can use for your development. With this feedback, you can ensure you purposefully build your brands to achieve your goals.

LISA'S STORY: The importance of external feedback

I just don't know what people think

During my time studying at Henley Business School, I had the great pleasure of coaching several people in the run-up to my certification in Executive Coaching.

Lisa had volunteered for regular coaching, as she was looking to further her career. We spent time reviewing her achievements and future goals. We also explored the obstacles that she felt would hold her back.

Lisa told me, 'One of my biggest worries is other people's opinions about me. It's hard to know what they really think.'

We had an opportunity to dig into this further in the coaching session, and I asked, 'What do people think of you? How are you soliciting feedback today, and how frequently?'

It turned out Lisa hadn't even asked for any feedback. Her self-critic had kicked in and had made some big assumptions about people's opinions of her work and capabilities.

After a little chuckle and the realisation that Lisa was potentially worrying unnecessarily, we quickly hatched a plan, using the technique below, to get some feedback for us to work with in future sessions.

Solicit feedback... regularly

While rushing around in our day-to-day lives, it's easy to forget to ask for feedback on our work, so we can understand our reputation and consider how we are perceived by our colleagues.

However, *guessing* what people think burns unnecessary emotional energy. It potentially sets you off in the wrong direction for solving issues that might not be a problem.

Structure feedback

Openly asking for feedback at work can be a scary prospect, so I'd like to recommend a tip I picked up from hearing the fabulous Carla Harris speak (I'll introduce you properly to Carla later in this book).

Carla recommends having three words that describe how you *want* other people to see you. This gives you the reputation you want to be known for. Carla then recommends a strategy and campaign to influence people to see you as those words.

My slight spin on this is to request feedback and ask people to describe you in three words – three-word feedback. You can then explore those words – good and bad – to understand why people see you in that way. This simplifies the feedback process because most people feel limited by the number so will consider the words carefully. There is also less chance they will include a negative word.

Bringing this back to a Personal Board: Imagine having people from whom you can *regularly* request feedback. They can also provide feedback on the progress you are making in changing others' perceptions of you.

It is always worthwhile taking time to check how people perceive you. All feedback is good for your development plan, as perception is key to progressing. A Personal Board is a routine sounding board.

These are just some ideas. In Chapters 8–10, I will provide some in-depth scenarios and sample agendas for working with your Personal Board.

Chapter review

You're never too young (or too old) to take control of your career. The Personal Board concept empowers you, encouraging and enabling you to make things happen rather than passively sitting back and waiting for your next career step.

Key takeaways

- Personal Boards are super-versatile. Whatever the stage of your career, a diverse group of connections will help you with advice and new perspectives on anything you want to achieve.

- A Personal Board encourages creative thinking – finding solutions you wouldn't previously have considered.

- There is a danger of thinking that, mid-career, you don't require any further input because you already know yourself and where you are heading. An extra pair of eyes helps by feeding back your strengths, weaknesses, suitability for a position, etc. Accessing critical but constructive feedback is a huge advantage and one that tends not to be delivered by organic advice.

- The extra pair of eyes doesn't necessarily have to belong to somebody more senior. In a management position with junior subordinates, it can be hugely informative to check in with younger people's beliefs, values and preferred ways of working.

- Career changes are now commonplace, and they necessitate an overhaul of your personal network. A Personal Board will help you settle into your new career much faster as well as take the fear out of making that change in the first place.

EXERCISE: Why change?

Review the scenarios and application ideas in this chapter for a Personal Board. Then continue to brainstorm:

- Which scenarios could you envisage using a Personal Board?
- How are your advisors working with you today?
- To accelerate progress, what extra skills or support might be useful?

Make notes for future chapters where we will explore these ideas further.

3
Corporate Building Blocks

It's vital to keep in mind at all times that your Personal Board is there to guide and advise, not to instruct or manipulate what you do. It should help to inform your decisions and open your eyes to opportunities, while the members stand back to ensure that all the decisions are ultimately yours.

What makes a corporate board successful

I've introduced the concept of the Personal Board and given a brief insight into how I first developed the concept. We're now going to take a look at real-life corporate boards and review the elements that make them successful. Once you know what 'good' looks like, it becomes far easier to visualise and apply the same to your situation.

In this chapter I've included what I consider to be the most important attributes of a good corporate board. For each attribute, I have included an explanation of how that principle can be easily transferred to the concept of a Personal Board.

Boards guide executives to achieve company objectives

A corporate board is there to help the executives deliver on the company's vision, mission and goals. The crucial word in that statement is *help* – it is the company's executives who set the goals and drive the day-to-day initiatives. The corporate board is there to guide, advise and govern the executives; to ensure that the company's goals are realistic, achievable and measurable; to consider the risks; and to track the company's progress against its goals.

This is a good way to think about your Personal Board. You are the CEO of your company, representing the company's executive team. You are the one who sets the goals and formulates the strategy of how to achieve them, and you are responsible for the day-to-day progress towards those goals. Your board is not there to do the work for you. They cannot achieve it for you. Your board can guide, advise and govern, to help you stay on track.

Boards provide accountability

A corporate board holds the executive team to account. Corporate boards are assembled to achieve company success – to ensure everyone is striving towards the targeted achievement.

In a corporate setting, if the company's executives had set goals and milestones, which the company subsequently failed to achieve, the board would be expected to review with the executives:

- Were the goals unrealistic?
- Was the market incorrectly assessed?
- Did any of the executives lack the necessary skills?
- Was the workforce motivated to achieve the goals?
- Were there any external mitigating factors?

Imagine you had spoken at length to a member of your Personal Board about applying for a new role, and the next time you met up with one of them, that person enquired, 'Did you apply for the role? How did it go?' Or perhaps you were an entrepreneur applying for funding and were subsequently asked by a member of your Personal Board, 'Did you apply for that funding?'

If you replied no to those questions, how do you think that would sit with your Personal Board after their investment in time with you? You might have a good reason, which would be accepted by your advisors, but what if you only had a lame excuse? What if you didn't apply for the role because you lacked confidence or missed the funding application deadline?

Verbalising goals to others, and those people holding you to account, is one of the key benefits of a Personal Board. Whatever goal you set, knowing that your board members will be checking in on your progress will give you extra motivation to achieve that goal.

PRIYA'S STORY: Creating new goals

Deliberating the next move

Priya had been working for her employer for five years as an individual contributor. She was ambitious and always looking for new projects to be working on. She was keen and had signed up for some diversity forums and working groups to supplement her skills and knowledge.

However, even though Priya was busy, she was bored. On her journey, she had somehow lost the love for the technical engineering role she had worked so hard for and, even though she had a fantastic reputation for being a go-to person, something was missing.

Through one of the company's diversity events, Priya met Matt, a senior manager within the business who had been studying for an MBA at Warwick University. Matt had been speaking on stage about opportunities for further development, which had piqued Priya's interest.

During the break, Priya went to meet Matt to discuss his MBA experience. She was particularly interested because Matt had outlined his journey, about how he had originally been a technical engineer and then progressed into senior management and become a student of company culture. By his own admission, he had been surprised by the change in his career.

Finding herself on common ground, Priya asked Matt for a follow-on conversation, and Matt subsequently became Priya's mentor for the next two years, giving her accountability for achieving new goals.

Priya described to me how it was Matt's honesty about his loss of passion that turned her head. While she didn't follow in his footsteps at Warwick University, she did enrol for an MBA at Henley Business School.

Priya has now left her company, founded her own start-up and volunteered to inspire young girls to study STEM subjects.

A Personal Board can advise, guide and inspire new ideas. However, the journey is always your own.

MY STORY: Learning to play the piano

The keys to success

Over the years, one of the best examples of my Personal Board holding me to account was in my learning to play the piano.

I had wanted to learn since I was little, but there were no lessons available in the schools I attended. As I grew up, I always promised myself that I would one day play the piano.

I happened to mention that intention to one of my board members, Nikki. I had told her the same a couple of times over several months but had made no progress.

The next time I saw Nikki, she asked me, 'So, when are you starting lessons?', which immediately sharpened my mind. It was January. I didn't own a piano. I hadn't found a teacher.

I was careful to make my response vague, replying, 'By Easter'.

After verbalising that deadline, my commitment to the goal increased ten-fold. I quickly sourced a piano and enquired about lessons. At the time of writing this, I am now three years into learning how to play. I know that, without Nikki's question or her encouragement to make the commitment, it would still be a dream.

Personal Board members will help to focus your mind on any of your goals and commitments.

In a corporate board, if commitments are missed, there will be an inquiry. Executives will be held to account, and they might even lose their place on the board.

On a Personal Board level, if you miss your commitments, you are unlikely to be kicked out! If this happens repeatedly, though, the people who you admire and trust are likely to stop offering you their time and advice.

Boards manage risk and deploy mitigation strategies

Corporate boards are there to avoid risk and to govern.

One of the principal responsibilities of a corporate board is to ensure that risks are fully assessed and subsequent mitigation strategies deployed, to safeguard the integrity of the company. These responsibilities are equally applicable to Personal Boards.

For example, say you are applying for a new job. There are many risk elements to consider, including:

- How you present yourself

- Whether you are qualified for the role

- If you have gaps in your experience

- Your competition and how you stack up against them

- How you can deploy strategies to focus on your strengths versus those of the competition

- What happens if you don't get the role

- What help you will need if you do get the role

- How you can put together your 90-day plan – the key activities and accomplishments you need to achieve in your first 90 days

This is where a few conversations with trusted advisors can help with the preparation for applying, interviewing and transitioning into the role. Perhaps some role-play scenarios and a few pertinent questions could help you with your initial interview preparation, while a strategy session to plan out your first moves would be useful once in the role.

On the flip side, what happens if you don't get the role? How will you feel? Will you stay with the company? What will you do next? These are all points a good Personal Board will consider, to help prepare you for all outcomes.

ANGELA'S STORY: Planning for promotion

Prep like a boss

Angela reached out to me at the beginning of 2022 when she was going for a promotion to technical manager in a company I had previously worked with.

She hadn't managed people before and was looking for advice on how she should approach the interview process and overcome the challenges of not having all of the perceived skills needed for the role.

After thirty minutes of conversation, we quickly established:

1. The interview process itself was unclear. This was driving anxiety. We didn't know how many steps, who was involved or how long it would take.
2. The hiring criteria were unclear. We didn't know the skills and capabilities needed for Angela to be seen as the number-one candidate for the role.

It's hard to play a game when you don't know the rules.

After Angela had taken down some actions and ideas, we then discussed who could help promote her for this position – who could provide the references and support that would nudge the stakeholders in her direction.

After forty-five minutes, Angela had compiled a campaign plan for her interview process, including support from influencers who could aid her cause and help her to:

- Confirm the nature of the interview process.
- Understand the stakeholders and their requirements.
- Gather references from key stakeholders to support the move.

This process might sound simple now, but often we need a little help to see the obvious.

Personal Board members will strategise with you. They may well also be able to provide references to help you achieve that next role.

Boards strategise with facts, not emotion

Corporate boards are single-minded in pursuit of their objectives.

When we discuss our careers and life goals, the stories we tell ourselves and others are often laced with emotion. Good corporate boards leave emotion at the door – facts, numbers and results are the order of the day.

This is useful on a personal level. Stepping outside of yourself and concentrating on the facts, ie, on what you know and don't know, ensures that you aren't adversely influenced by the stories in your head, the hearsay or the office gossip. Instead, you can concentrate on working with the facts and create strategies to understand what you don't know.

When you apply for a new role or enter a transition period, it's easy to make assumptions or even distort reality. The world is a fast-moving, emotional place, so it's important to take the time to stop and think about what is real. Taking time with one of your advisors allows you to pause for breath and to consider the reality of your situation.

If chosen wisely, your Personal Board members will be slightly removed from your situation, so they can be naturally objective, in the same way that a non-executive board director is there to provide an independent voice.

AMRITA'S STORY: Establishing the facts

Eliminating distortion and fine-tuning the feedback

Amrita was a sales executive in a software company who was up for a promotion to country manager. She asked me for some advice to practise her pitch ahead of her big interview.

When we practised role play, I quickly realised that her arguments for the promotion were emotionally charged. Amrita had limited facts and figures to provide evidence of her track record or success, which could help the interviewer understand her capabilities for the future role.

I shared this feedback with Amrita, and we quickly changed tack to brainstorming key facts and figures that would provide evidence of her knowledge and capability for the role.

We also removed any distortions from her campaign, such as Amrita being the only qualified person going for the role. When we discussed this, Amrita realised she had not considered the potential appointment of an outside candidate. Her distortion had discounted any competition, which could have made her unprepared for the interview.

The chance of an outside appointment was also very real. We discussed how Amrita would feel if she was unsuccessful to an outside candidate. What would be the risk to her mindset in staying loyal to the company? Could she be open to such a scenario?

A short brainstorm later, considering all the arguments and perspectives, Amrita was ready to embark on the interview process.

Personal Board members are there to keep us grounded and objective.

Boards respectfully challenge

You don't need any yes-men (or yes-women) on your Personal Board.

If you consider the worst boards in corporate history, their refusal or inability to challenge the most influential executives was their downfall. Think of Enron (fraud), Barings (fraud) and BP (safety). With any of these corporate failures, there have been signals to the board that something untoward was going on in the company. Sometimes these were innocent mistakes. Often there was a lack of confidence on the part of the executives to speak up. Invariably, there was a dominant personality involved.

The board's role is to keep the company on the straight and narrow – to keep it true to its internal goals, while understanding and assessing the external risks. If the board is not satisfied with the answers from its executives, it needs to respectfully challenge the executive team and explore their perspectives and opinions.

The key here is to *respectfully* challenge. For Personal Boards, this is equally important. Your Personal Board is not there to criticise you, disagree with you or force you to change your strategy. It is there to provide checks and balances, to advise on alternative perspectives and to ensure that you have considered the alternatives. The respect here should work both ways – you should value their checks and their perspectives, you should thank them for their opinions, and you should ensure you consider their counsel.

SARAH'S STORY: The only promotion is in another company

The green, green grass of home

Sarah had been an individual contributor for almost ten years, having spent five years with her current employer. She was now interested in a promotion, and she also understood that she needed to develop herself. When an external offer of promotion arose, along with a pay rise and development opportunities, it all sounded perfect.

Sarah called me for a catch-up. 'It's a great opportunity,' she said. 'Development, promotion, pay rise... just what I'm looking for.'

Impartial to the move, and acutely aware that the grass is not always greener on the other side, I asked Sarah whether she had spoken with her existing company about matching the opportunity: 'Have you asked your company for the same type of promotion?'

I was prompted to ask this because I knew Sarah loved her current boss. They had built a great relationship, and Sarah understood how rare this support could be in the world of sales. This was why she had been having doubts and seeking counsel.

I continued, asking Sarah what she had to lose by asking for the match. If the new opportunity was so great and she was leaving anyway, then what did it matter?

Sarah took my advice and asked her boss for the same opportunity, and what do you think happened? You guessed it – they matched the offer, and Sarah was promoted, given a pay rise and the same personal development opportunity, with less risk and a great boss.

It was a win–win for everybody.

Personal Board members can shine a light on other options and choices.

The diversity of corporate boards

I have outlined how good corporate boards operate and how these qualities can be translated into an effective Personal Board. There is one remaining aspect of the success of the highest-achieving boards: diversity.

Boards are assembled with people of different levels and types, to cover all angles when governing a company. Historically, though, this has focused on diversity of skills and experience.

In the twenty-first century, there has been a concerted effort to increase the diversity of corporate boards, away from the traditional preserve of the white, upper-class male. Why? The more diverse the board, the better the company will be governed and the faster it will grow.

BACKGROUND INFORMATION: Diversity wins

- 'Companies with the best gender diversity in their executive teams were more likely to have above-average profitability.
- The more a company improves on its ethnic and cultural diversity, the more profitable it becomes.
- It's not enough only to hire for diversity – the workplace experience makes the biggest difference.'

Source: 'Diversity wins: How inclusion matters', McKinsey & Company

---

Companies lacking diversity are being left behind. More diverse boards make better decisions. The same applies to Personal Boards.

I have talked about what our Personal Boards can offer us and that diverse advice and opinions achieve better results. Diversity is important in every sense – culture, race, religion, experience, skills, gender, age, sexual persuasion and so on.

If you are taking the time to purposefully assemble the best and brightest people to accelerate your achievement, you must ensure diversity is at the heart of your selection process.

Chapter review

This chapter discussed the parallels between a corporate board and a Personal Board, to help guide you in creating the most effective group of people to help with your goals.

Key takeaways

- Boards will guide and advise; they cannot do the job for you. Take their advice and execute the hard yards to achieve your goal.

- Boards must be able to respectfully challenge. Two-way respect is imperative to enable transparent working relationships with those who advise you. Both sides need to be able to speak up when aware of the wrong decision or course of action.

- Diversity wins the day – every single time (because there is never actually enough said about diversity).

EXERCISE: Consider the benefits past and future

Consider the parallels between a corporate board and a Personal Board, then reflect on these questions:

- Are you using your Personal Board to challenge you today?
- What elements of diversity are there within your current advisors, and what is needed?
- How regularly are you engaging with advisors with structured agendas?

4
Guiding Principles

Before you select this amazing group of people who make up your Personal Board, let's consider some of the guiding principles that will keep you on the straight and narrow.

In this chapter, I'll look at the need for the three guiding principles of any Personal Board: a respected group of people, with whom you have regular contact, and whose advice you will carefully consider (even if you end up not acting on that advice).

The Personal Board concept is an extremely simple one – that's what makes it so effective. It's highly flexible, extremely individualistic and remarkably quick to set up.

The following guiding principles are so important that they deserve this whole chapter to highlight their importance. Should you ever be concerned about any advice you are receiving, please refer back to these three principles. They can be used to address any concerns.

First principle: Trust and respect

You are going to be sharing a great deal of your external self with your Personal Board: your career plans, your goals and your aspirations. You will also share a fair amount of your inner self: your reflections, your thoughts and your insecurities.

With respect comes trust. If you're not prepared to share all the details of your current situation – the context, your motivations and what makes you tick – the chances are that you'll omit some relevant information, which will result in deficient advice from your Personal Board.

Transparency and vulnerability are needed, to present *all* the facts, so that any external advice can objectively drive the best outcomes. This will require a leap of faith, since some of the people you identify as new board members will start off as relative strangers.

MY STORY: Unsolicited, biased advice

Not choosing wisely

In the beginning, when I shared a little about my own story, I talked about the time I decided to move roles from Sun Microsystems to BMC Software.

I'd already signed the contract to leave Sun, and the news was out among the team. About a day or so after the announcement, one of the Sun managers came to ask me about my move.

'Are you absolutely sure about this? You're doing really well at Sun, and I don't feel this move is the best thing for you.'

I was a little surprised, as I hadn't previously had much interaction with this particular manager, and I certainly hadn't shared any of my plans or future aspirations with him.

After some further chat, it turned out the manager knew the individuals I was going to work for, 'Hey, I know these guys. I'm not sure this is the right environment for you'.

Slightly taken aback, I mulled this over for the rest of the day. When I returned home that evening, that exchange sparked the Personal Board conversation around my kitchen table.

I later discovered that when this manager had previously worked with my future employers, there had been some strong views on both sides about each other's capabilities. As I reflected on the unsolicited advice I realised a couple of things:

1. The advice was unsolicited and from a source I did not trust. Frankly, I didn't know the guy well at all, which prompted me to check out the context.

2. The advice was based on that manager's idea of what 'good' meant for me – based on his own experiences and goals rather than being focused on my goals.

As it turned out, my time at BMC was hugely successful and I learned a lot from the team there. Of course, it wasn't easy or without its challenges, but learning from that experience made it a journey worth taking.

Organic advice is often coloured by other people's experiences and their ignorance of your specific situation. Purposefully creating a Personal Board with people you respect and trust will ensure you share the relevant information and can receive the most rounded advice.

As always, the final decision on the level of transparency rests with you, especially as to what constitutes the appropriate level of information-sharing. For example, when talking to a senior person or relative stranger, you might choose to give a précis of the core facts and a high-level view of what you're aiming to achieve. With a mentor or old friend, you'll have a more in-depth conversation and share your feelings about a situation.

What defines a respected person?

One of the biggest stumbling blocks when establishing a Personal Board for the first time is the tendency to only consider long-standing friends and colleagues as respected or trustworthy. This can restrict your Personal Board's future development to the point where it ceases to be objective.

There are several factors to consider when identifying respected contacts as potential Personal Board members.

Confidentiality

You will be talking about personal plans and sharing vulnerabilities, so you must be confident the conversation will remain confidential. I know some great people who can provide great advice, but if it came to deeper issues, I would be more selective about what I told them, based on issues of confidentiality.

We now live in a world that is so connected, it's easy to let slip information that could negatively impact your journey. You *need* to feel confident that your Personal Board member can keep a secret.

Impartiality

Board members need to be able to take time to understand and listen, and their advice should be unbiased, practical and considerate. If you regularly received biased, unrealistic or reckless advice, it would simply be a waste of everyone's time.

There may well be times when you disagree with the advice given, but overall, you must feel that the person providing the advice has your best interests at heart.

Integrity

Admiring the achievements of others might attract you to recruit those people as new members. However, you first need to be sure you understand *how* they achieved their successes.

Integrity is a good marker for Personal Board members – look for people who have signs of honesty and humility in their backstory. Also, don't forget people junior to you. When establishing your Personal Board, be sure that you are taking advice from younger people as well as older, more tenured individuals. People in the earlier phases of their careers, including those in different industries, can provide vital alternative perspectives.

A respected source needs to have your best interests at heart, which means that confidentiality and how they conduct themselves are key. This is all well and good, but how would you know all of this in advance with a stranger?

Respect and trust with strangers

One of the distinctions of a Personal Board – purposefully seeking people for new connections – is to extend your reach, knowledge and opportunities in any industry. You might therefore be wondering how you can establish early trust with people you don't know.

The best way to overcome 'stranger danger' is, again, by properly using your network. If you carefully ask your network for new connections, they will invariably connect you with trusted people in *their* network.

You'll need to take the time to explain to the people in your network what you need and why you are looking for certain connections. To be able to ask for this favour, you will have to have built strong relationships in your network and be confident that the outcome will be successful. The trust is then implicit on both sides. If your network is sound, the people you ask will not want to let you – or the new connection – down with a bad experience.

Asking a relative stranger to connect you to another relative stranger will usually yield poor results. Similarly, if you don't take the time to brief your connection properly, it's likely that you won't make a good connection with their introduction.

Asking for a connection from a strong, trusted person, who is well-briefed and who understands your needs, will usually deliver the best results.

MY STORY: Expanding your Personal Board

In search of Eastern promise

When I joined Ping Identity in 2020, as general manager for the international business, I hadn't previously worked in many countries outside of the UK. I needed to quickly get to grips with the Asian marketplace.

Using my existing network, I mapped out six strong contacts who had previously worked in the Asian marketplace, and focused on spending time with them to increase my knowledge of those markets. After an initial conversation, I spent some time sharing a little of my knowledge gap and then asked for their help.

It's worth noting that I had significantly invested in these relationships in the past. Most were senior heads of tech businesses, with whom I had shared past successes or senior customer contacts.

After I shared some thoughts about the problem and the help that I needed, they happily shared their knowledge, context and senior connections to further develop my network in the region. After some initial conversations, I established two key relationships with people who became long-term mentors, helping to grow my knowledge of the Asian marketplace.

This is an example of using a Personal Board for a specific project or event. Those six people may, or may not, feature in the long term on my Personal Board. However, certainly, for the duration of this project, they were great assets in helping me achieve my immediate goals.

An existing network can extend your reach to new, trusted connections to add to your Personal Board.

Second principle: Regular engagement

Going back to the parallels with a corporate board: Those board members meet regularly to keep things shipshape. Similarly, as you move away from ad hoc advice and look to use your Personal Board strategically and for progression, you need to establish regular contact.

Regular contact doesn't necessarily mean every day, every week or even every month, but it also doesn't mean once in a blue moon. The ideal frequency of contact depends on the Personal Board member and how they are relevant to your goals. You will naturally speak with some more often than others at different stages of your progress.

By establishing regular contact, you can keep pace with your goals, your thinking and your commitment to your plan. If you go too long without talking to your Personal Board members, they might forget the context of your story or miss an important development in your career, so set a reminder or diarise to check in with each member, even if only for a chat.

Third principle: Guidance and advice

Their advice, your decision

Your Personal Board is your 'brains trust' – your advisory council. It's there to guide you, advise you and bring you a fresh perspective. The keyword here, though, is *guidance* – it's ultimately your choice which path you choose.

The downside of organic advisors

One of the pitfalls of organically gathering advisors is that you will often be taking advice from people who have a vested interest in your career path.

If you take a moment to think about people you currently ask for advice, I imagine they will include some of the following characters:

- **Peers:** People striving for the same promotions/pay rises as yourself

- **Senior staff:** People you work for or who have a stake in your success

- **Business partners:** Those with whom you have joint business interests

- **Your life partner:** The person with whom you share financial and personal goals

I am not suggesting you need to go out in search of completely impartial people, but it's important to ensure there is a balance among your advisors. Guiding and advising should be about helping you evaluate your options, but it's your path, your choice and your plan. You need to limit any possibility of manipulation for others' gain.

MAX'S STORY: Their advice, your decision

The voices in my head

Max is an entrepreneur I've worked with from time to time. When Max first started his software business in 2020, it consisted only of Max and two close employees. As the business developed and became a proper start-up with outside investment, other industry experts arrived on the scene to help push it forward.

Early in 2021, just before the next round of investment, Max suddenly hit a tipping point. He had moved from taking measured advice from two or three people to suddenly having around fifteen people constantly bombarding him with advice, whether he wanted it or not.

Of that group of advisors, most were invested in the business, so every piece of advice was based on their motivations and not the goals set out by the CEO and founder.

The path had become unclear for Max, as he now had a lot of people telling him what he should be doing with the business, and all the advice conflicted with his own goals.

My advice to Max was as follows:

'As the CEO, your role is to seek advice, to ask for help and to solicit opinions from as many people as you can. However, as CEO, you are ultimately the person who must sort through everything and decide the best path for you and the company.

'Your role also needs you to see others' interests in the business and ensure you filter out any advice that doesn't achieve your goals.'

An organic group of advisors can grow quickly and fundamentally have their own goals at heart. Seek advice and guidance from unbiased sources. Boards are there to advise. Listen to their advice and then make your own decisions.

Your Personal Board is there to help, but just like a corporate board, it's down to the executives to make the final decision. In the case of You Inc., you are the CEO, so be confident in your decision-making and don't worry about taking a different path. It's your expertise and judgement that should set you apart.

You are responsible for choosing whether to act on the advice you receive.

Chapter review

This chapter has laid the foundations for your Personal Board by examining the guiding principles you can come back to, to ensure you are maximising the network and team around you.

Key takeaways

- Ensure you have respect and trust with Personal Board members.
  - If in doubt, consider the source of the advice. Seek out respected board members who can provide considered advice.

- Maintain regular engagement.
  - Consider how you will keep your Personal Board members in the loop about progress.
  - For every key conversation, ensure you make time for follow-ups to retain those board members.

- Be cautious of influence.
  - Carefully consider any advice before acting on it – it has to be your decision.
  - Exercise caution if you feel a board member has something to gain. Your board should be there for you, and only you.

EXERCISE: Initial planning

Reflect on this chapter and start to consider:

- How could you extend beyond your immediate trusted network?
- Who are the three people who could connect you to other 'experts' and advisors?
- What specific goals would you ask these people to help with?

5
Starting With Your Objectives

Before you can get started with practical advice on growing your Personal Board, it's imperative you set out what you are hoping to achieve. Personal Boards are great at creating options for you, but you first need to choose something to talk about, typically using your development plan.

When I was starting in my career, the trend was to undergo SWOT (strengths, weaknesses, opportunities, threats) analysis as part of any personal development plan and to develop career goals accordingly. Over time, I have come to focus less on my flaws and more on my passions and strengths. If you follow your heart and direct your energy accordingly, you are more likely to stay motivated to achieve your development goals.

This chapter will outline objectives around your development, which can be the focus of your efforts with a Personal Board. This is by no means an extensive chapter on goal setting – there are many books out there that cover that in greater detail. It does relate, though, to the points in Chapter 10 about the need for your board members to see some progress in return for their time. Before you can give that feedback, you need to be clear on what you need from them.

Personal objective brainstorm

To establish the most relevant Personal Board, you first need to define your destination. The objectives or goals you set for your development will then determine the actions and people needed to cross the finish line. For example, if your goal is to swim the English Channel, it's no good having a Personal Board comprising only corporate executives – you might want to consider a swimming coach first!

Setting objectives doesn't need to be perfect. They will also likely change over time, but it's important to start somewhere and have a few thoughts written down. I'm not a believer in personal development plans that take months to build and end up becoming so onerous that the process of goal setting ends up hindering any practical progress.

As reassurance: It's natural not to be sure about your next objective. I often meet people who, after we start talking about Personal Boards, confide, 'I've got no idea what my next career step is,' or 'I have so many choices, and I am trying to work out which path is best.' They feel that something is not quite right with their career, but don't know what's missing.

In this section, I will cover some quick and easy ways to brainstorm where you are today and some ideas to help you identify new areas for development. If you already have a personal development plan, great – feel free to skip to Step 4: Defining three objectives or goals you need help with.

To arrive at a basic plan for your direction, I will run through a quick, four-step process so you can design a Personal Board accordingly.

The steps will be:

1. **Recognising your future state**

   This is all about considering what might be different in the future for you, personally and professionally.

2. **Identifying your happiest workdays and potential passions**

   This will help you identify how you like to spend your time and give insights to feed back to your future state.

3. **Considering possible paths**

   This is about possible paths to achieving your future state – perhaps with parallel projects or choices.

4. **Defining three objectives or goals you need help with**

   Here you will pick three next steps you will strive towards, for which you can ask for help from your Personal Board.

Step 1: Recognising your future state

To get started, think first about how you would like your future state to look. Don't agonise over perfecting your ideas – simply brainstorm and let everything flow. Your future state is about where and how would you like to be in the future.

For example, if something could be different, what would this be?

- I'd like to move house. Why? For more space for my family.

- I'd like to work less. Why? To have more time to focus on my painting.

- I'd like to travel less for work. Why? To be able to spend more time with my family.

When you are brainstorming these ideas, think both personally and professionally. Also, try to use words that add emotion to your thoughts. The 'Why?' should help spark some emotion, but think about how you could visualise the future to make it more real for you.

Below, I have listed a few prompts to help you think about your new future state. Use these prompts to brainstorm and make some initial notes.

Prompts

Personal goals and passions

- Do you have some personal goals, eg related to travel, health or family?

- What are your passions?

- What would you like to do more (or less)?

- Is there something you've always wanted to achieve but have never started?

Family and friends

- How would you like to change things with your family or friends?

Environments

- Would you like to change anything about how and where you work today?

- How do you spend your days and how would you like to change that?

- Who would you like to spend more (or less) time with?

Financial

- How are you set financially? Anything to change?

- How does your financial situation reflect how you would like to be in the future?

- Are there any changes you would like to see?

Professional

- Is there a professional future state you would like to achieve?

- Do you yearn for a certain status, accreditation or company?

- Do you crave some level of recognition or accolade?

When brainstorming these ideas, try to stay away from career definitions, as you may find this limits your thinking. Initially, simply visualise how you would like to *be* in the future. This is less about the job title and more about your identity and how you are every day.

Step 2: Identifying your happiest workdays and potential passions

Often, when I ask people about their passions, some have never articulated theirs out loud. This is often a product of the environments we work in today. Our passions often conflict with the work we are doing or with the egos around us, so we keep them hidden.

It's important to recognise that your passions are your motivators, delivering your happiest workdays.

Think about what makes you jump out of bed early in the morning. Is there a theme in the stories you tell at home about why you love your work? Think back over the last few months. Remember a day when you skipped in through the front door after your day at work feeling happy, fulfilled and excited to share the day's events. What made that day so great? What are the activities or environments you thrive in?

Thinking about your happiest days will give you insight into how you want to achieve your goals. Being 'in flow' and thriving in your everyday environment will help your motivation and your drive to achieve the objectives and goals you set out to accomplish.

Think now about your happiest times. Use the prompts below and make notes on all the following points.

Prompts

Where you were

- Work

- Home

- Location

- Other

Who you were with

- Friends

- Colleagues

- Large group

- Small group

- Alone

What you were doing

- Presenting

- Brainstorming

- Project-based work

- Helping others

- Other

What role you were playing

- The expert

- The student

- The teammate

- The leader

- Other

Was there anything else about the activity or environment you remember as being enjoyable?

After you have made some notes, check your list. Are there any particular points that stand out for you and make you smile? These are likely to be close to the heart of your passions – the environments you thrive in most. Take careful note, as those will help formulate the next steps.

Step 3: Considering possible paths

Now you need to think about the possible paths, journeys and achievements you would like to see in your future. Understanding this is all part of your personal development – it will provide you with goals to strive for and areas to explore on your journey. These will be the goals you wrap your Personal Board around to help you get there faster.

This is where you need to think more specifically about what you would like to be or achieve. Think about the possible job titles, roles and career options you have in mind for the future.

Prompts

Personal achievements

- Buy a house
- Start a business
- Run a marathon
- Volunteer for a charity
- Retire early
- Other

Professional achievements

- Get a promotion or two
- Improve your reputation in an industry
- Become a more comfortable public speaker
- Broaden your experience, moving from executive to board
- Other

These high-level prompts are there to stimulate your initial thinking. Ideally, you want to arrive at something more specific, along the following lines:

- Swim the English Channel
- Join the board of Refuge
- Develop knowledge of the Asian tech market
- Get a mentor on conducting business in Germany
- Achieve a promotion to team leader
- Obtain a master's degree in…

Recommendation

Once you have a few ideas written down, this is a great first exercise to brainstorm for thirty minutes with existing Personal Board members, friends, colleagues or mentors.

Our own ideas are shaped by our knowledge, our experience and our exposure to different opportunities.

More people = more knowledge = more experience and exposure to other ideas.

Step 4: Defining three objectives or goals you need help with

Now you have some ideas about what you'd like to achieve in the future, your Personal Board is going to help you accelerate those achievements by:

1. Helping to develop your knowledge in a new area, so you can gain experience faster

2. Connecting you to people in that field who can provide opportunities

3. Coaching and guiding you in your strategy to achieve

Your goal now is to start broadening your contacts and connections to help you achieve your goals.

The power of three

As I mentioned before, I believe in keeping development plans simple. Progress can be easily defined and quick to achieve. Start small, making your development plan short and achievable.

A great way to do this is to focus on the power of three, whether that's three new connections, three goals or three actions. The power of three will keep plans achievable and the pace quick.

Examples of objectives and next steps

To link your objectives to your next steps, I have provided a few examples below of how these might be connected.

Objectives	Next step ideas
Swim the English Channel	Find a swimming coach
	Find a mentor who has achieved this
	Research a nutritionist
Work in Asia	Find a mentor who has worked in Asia
	Connect with local recruiters for new hires
	Locate a mentor in the local area
Join a corporate board	Find a mentor who made this journey
	Connect to organisations that can help
	Connect to a recruiter in this space

Once you have made notes on your objectives and next steps, you can start to think about quick wins for establishing your Personal Board. Keep referring to your objectives throughout this process to ensure that as you plan while building your board, the right connections are in place alongside you.

Your plan

Once you have completed all of the steps, you should end up with a short and snappy plan such as in the example below. This will help you as you move into identifying and increasing your Personal Board members in the next chapter.

Example: Caroline's personal development plan

Notes on today	• Fifty-three years old
	• Full-time accountant working for XYZ company; tenure of fifteen years
	• Leading a team of seven people
	• Interested in coaching others and learning something new but limited time to achieve this
Future state	Personal
	• Want more time to study and travel
	• Need to keep earning to fund my study and travel
	Professional
	• Move from full-time accountancy to a more consultative career
	• Offer some pro bono time to charities
Passions/happiest days	• I *love* to coach. Helping people with their careers gives me a buzz. I enjoy studying and learning more about the subject too.
	• Travel – all my family love to travel. It also helps me to relax.
	• People – my best days are with lots of people.
Paths and options	• Could I study coaching? What would this involve? Where would I go for this? Costs?
	• Should I offer pro bono coaching?
	• Could I offer my services to a charity? How would this work? What role would I take?

	• Could I become a full-time coach? What would this entail? How quickly could I set myself up? Do I need to consider my finances?
	• Are there options to coach within my company – less risk?
Next steps	• Find a mentor who knows the coaching world.
	• Explore best options for coaching courses – recommendations?
	• Connect with some charities to explore pro bono options.

Chapter review

This chapter has covered brainstorming quick ways to create your personal development plan and consider personal development goals, and how you can build your Personal Board to help you towards your goals.

Key takeaways

- Before deciding on your ideal Personal Board members, define objectives and goals for your development. You don't need to spend ages creating the perfect plan – it can be a simple document listing your initial thoughts, which you will continue to develop.

- Your passions are your motivators, delivering your happiest workdays. Thinking about your happiest days will give you insight into how you want to achieve your goals.

- Understanding the possible paths, journeys and achievements you would like to see in your future provides you with goals to strive for and areas to explore on your journey. Once you have a list, reduce it to three key connections, goals or actions, which will accelerate your success in those areas.

EXERCISE: Connect your board and goals

Review the planning process contained in this chapter:

- Create three goals to focus your Personal Board on.
- Brainstorm who is best aligned to help with each goal.
- Consider who outside of your immediate network could be recruited to help too.

6

Building Your
Personal Board

Whenever I share the process for a Personal Board, I keep it to four key steps:

1. Identify your needs.

2. Build your board.

3. Use your board.

4. Feed back to the board.

In this chapter I will cover the first of these points: Identifying your needs, ie, identifying the types of people you need to connect with to help you reach your goals. Make notes on your thoughts and ideas as you go through this chapter. It will help you to refer back to your notes later, remind yourself of ideas and recognise the progress you've made.

Identify your needs

Your current Personal Board: Organic members

Your organic conversations and connections have stood you in great stead up to this point, and you shouldn't forget the fantastic support that they have provided. You will have no doubt collected some great advisors along the way, who will continue to be a great support going forward.

EXERCISE: Your existing Personal Board

Reviewing your notes from the last chapter, take a minute to consider your current advisors:

- Who you regularly approach for advice
- Who you discuss career progression or new business ideas with
- Why you go to these people for advice
- What they bring to the party, for example, expertise, knowledge, networks, experience

Think about your relationship with each of these people – what is their role? Are they a coach, mentor, peer, industry connection, spouse or friend?

This exercise will give you something like this list:

Fred

- Finance expert
- Knows me personally
- Spouse

Sarah

- Provides good advice
- Friend for twenty years

Tom

- High-achieving executive
- My CEO/sponsor
- Has charity connections

Millie

- Ex-investment banker
- Wide network
- Ex-colleague for five years

Now you have made notes on people you already go to for help and advice, you need to think about what you are missing.

Gap analysis

The whole idea behind the Personal Board is to help you get to your next destination faster. If you stay in your comfort zone, asking the same people for advice and help, your career progress will be slower.

Before you start thinking about the names of the people you want to consult, you need to conduct a gap analysis exercise to pinpoint what you need for your Personal Board.

If you refer to the notes you made in Chapter 5, you should have already written down some goals for your Personal Board, along with any next steps. Now you need to review the people you currently approach for advice, to see whether they will help you going forward.

I've provided an example below of a Personal Board list based on the fictional personal development plan from Chapter 5. I have listed the names and attributes of the Personal Board members as well as my objectives, and I have also identified a couple of possible connections in the paragraph that follows the table.

Fred	*Sarah*
Finance expert	Provides good advice
Knows me personally	Friend for twenty years
Spouse	
Tom	*Millie*
High-achieving/executive	Ex-investment banker
My CEO/sponsor	Wide network
Has charity connections	Ex-colleague for five years

My objectives

Find a mentor for coaching

Recommendations for coaching courses

Charities – pro bono help?

My CEO contact and sponsor, Tom, has several charity connections and may be able to help with ideas on how I can connect with them. As a senior executive, he is also likely to know coaches who specialise in helping senior executives.

As previously mentioned, once you start to think purposefully about using your network to achieve things, it should come as no surprise that you find you already have useful connections in place. Crucial, though, is whether your existing network provides the *right* advice, knowledge and future connections.

EXERCISE: Advanced gap analysis

Consider your goals for a few moments. Beyond the initial goal, you have already detailed, what additional help do you think you might need in the future?

Here is an example of how to brainstorm ideas around a goal:

Goal: Find a mentor for coaching

- What sort of coaching would you like to go into?
- What sort of coach would you like to connect with?
- What are some of the skills gaps you would like the mentor to help you with? For example:
  - Setting up a coaching business – financial/ business support?
  - How to access the best training – coaching/ educational support?
  - How to position yourself in the market and gain new clients – sales support?
- Are you looking for an experienced mentor or someone who has just begun mentoring and has a fresh perspective? What tenure are you looking for in your mentor?

With this exercise, you are brainstorming and gathering ideas to assess the gaps in your current knowledge and to imagine what an ideal Personal Board contact might look like. This also helps you think about your connections, enabling you to make a more refined choice for your next connection, thereby increasing your chances of success.

Make some notes on your goals from Chapter 5 and qualify exactly what you are looking for from your Personal Board members.

Once you have detailed your precise requirements, you can look at your existing Personal Board members and consider whether they can help you with your journey.

PRACTICAL TIP: Don't settle – You don't need to

If your original advisors have been fantastic helpers in the past, it's common (and easier) to go to the same people in the future. However, don't settle for their advice out of loyalty.

Your existing Personal Board wants what is best for you. If there is a better-suited, more knowledgeable contact in the industry who can help you, I am certain they would be happy to connect with you.

It's also important to remember that your Personal Board will evolve and, if your journey happens to take a different path, the people advising you today may not be the ones advising you in the future. That's OK too.

> People may leave and return at a later date. Just ensure you are honest with your Personal Board members about your needs and when you will next speak to them.

With this advice in mind, look again at your goals and your existing Personal Board. What are you missing? What advice could you improve on? Are there better connections available in your network, just a hop or two away?

Diversity dimensions

If you seek five opinions from people with the same backgrounds, education, skill sets and motivations, you are likely to get the same advice from them all and probably only one angle on how to tackle an issue.

If you take a group of people with diverse backgrounds and perspectives, their collective wisdom is more likely to drive a better outcome.

> **BACKGROUND INFORMATION: The wisdom of the crowds**
>
> A 2013 *National Geographic* article describes how in the early 1900s, Sir Francis Galton (an eminent statistician and polymath) attended a village fair in Plymouth, where a competition was taking place to guess the weight of an ox. Almost 800 people

entered the competition, but nobody managed to guess the correct weight.

However, when Galton averaged all of their guesses, he arrived at an almost perfect estimate. In fact, it was under by only 1 lb, for an ox that weighed 1,198 lb. This collective guess was not only better than the actual winner of the contest but also better than all the guesses made by the cattle experts at the fair.

There was a phrase coined for this collective intelligence: 'The wisdom of the crowds'.

PRACTICAL TIP: How big a crowd?

I am by no means suggesting that anyone needs a Personal Board consisting of 800 people. For me, the optimum number is six to eight people at any one time.

This allows for the group to be large enough to create options for diversity, and small enough that communication and regular engagement with a feedback loop are manageable.

Remember that each board member will require regular meetings and updates. However, you also have your life to live.

Review the effectiveness of your board at least quarterly. Have your goals changed? Do you need people with new skills or perspectives? (see Chapter 8 for more tips.)

Thinking about diversity as a key part of your Personal Board does take some planning. Unfortunately, bias is inherent in all of us to varying degrees, which is something you need to be conscious of when thinking about the composition of your Personal Board. To achieve diversity, you need to take yourself out of your comfort zone.

I have listed some of the key diversity elements to consider. This is by no means an exhaustive list, so please think of it only as a starting point:

- Background

- Work experience

- Skillset: soft and hard skills

- Education

- Gender

- Age/seniority

- Thought: neurodiversity

As you consider each diversity element in turn, keep referring to your current Personal Board to highlight the similarities or differences in your board members.

Background

Our upbringing drives our beliefs, our values and our views. In short: It forms the basis of who we are.

If your goal is to seek new perspectives, then having people from different backgrounds on your Personal Board will broaden your outlook and allow you to see things from a variety of angles – geographically, culturally and politically.

Remember: If you are aiming for true diversity to obtain a 360° view, then you need to have a full range of people – from backgrounds similar to as well as different from your own.

Work experience

By work experience, I am referring to the professional career paths your Personal Board members have taken. This is not to be confused with seniority, which is covered later in this chapter.

Thinking about your board members:

- Where have they worked?
- Did they take a conventional path to their current role?
- In what range of seniority levels have they worked?

Somebody with an entrepreneurial, self-employed or small-business background will have a different perspective from that of a graduate who left university, went to work for a large corporation and has stayed there ever since.

Skill set: Soft and hard skills

Skill set refers to the entire range of an individual's skills, experience and abilities. It encompasses both soft skills (qualitative and non-measurable, such as communication ability) as well as hard skills (quantitative and measurable, such as financial knowledge).

Your skill set is particularly important as you move into leadership and are looking to develop skills that cannot be learned from a textbook but that need to be observed, to drive inspiration and learning.

This category is particularly interesting for entrepreneurs, founders and those about to move into a new role. In those scenarios, you'll probably be thinking about knowledge and skills you don't have and how others can help fill those gaps.

LAURA'S STORY: Angel to entrepreneur

Corporate to start-up transition

I met Laura about four years ago. We have both been long-standing members of Angel Academe, which invests in female-founded businesses.

When I met Laura, she had just exited a super-successful corporate career, having been director of digital projects at Selfridges. The corporate ladder hadn't been an easy one for her, with plenty of twists and turns along the way.

After leaving Selfridges, Laura became an advisor, a non-executive director and an angel investor.

Enjoying her portfolio career, one day Laura had an epiphany while in the supermarket. Already deeply concerned about climate change and the prospects for the world that her children would inherit, Laura was inspired to make a change of direction when faced with the selection of wholly unsustainable cleaning products available on the supermarket shelves.

Using her background and knowledge of the retail industry, Laura quickly established a niche for some key products that would make up Seep, a 100% plastic-free, sustainable cleaning products business.

While Laura was an accomplished retail executive, she is the first to confess that starting her own eco-friendly start-up was not in her core skill set. She quickly needed to consider help on how to make a success of her newly founded business.

Laura's network, built over many years, quickly began to bear fruit:

- **Corporate colleagues**

  The first port of call was Laura's ex-colleagues from the Selfridges world. What insights and experience could they provide on supply chain and retail?

- **Angel network**

  The support of the angel investment network provided a huge range of different types of business experience, which Laura could use to develop her idea into a faster-growing business. Furthermore, Laura's investor background had exposed her to so many business ideas, pitches, accounts and founders that she had a finely tuned entrepreneurial compass on how start-ups succeeded or failed – invaluable experience for when she became the fundraiser.

- **Founder network**

  Most people want to help and share their experiences to see others succeed. Laura found that sharing her idea with several founders in the network allowed those founders an opportunity to help her, in the same way as she had helped them in their early days. Those founders quickly became Laura's new peer group, offering regular help and support as she embarked on her journey.

The result from the network was fantastic. Laura learned the soft skills of running a start-up business as well as how to get investors onboard and excited. She also gained the hard skills of day-to-day business management and ensuring the business had the sufficient runway to grow, which is particularly important in such a tough macroeconomic environment.

Diverse networks provide a multitude of soft and hard skills, which can be called on as you change direction in your life and career.

Once again, you need to look for new ways to view the same problems, based on other people's expertise.

Education

Degree or no degree? MBA or PhD? Or maybe just the university of life? People with an academic background tend to have a different perspective from those who started work early with no or limited qualifications. Working from a young age can make you more reactive than reflective, with a need to do things straight away, conscious of the pressures of work, demands and deadlines. On the other hand, those who have studied to a higher degree level have been taught to think from an academic perspective and to have a longer-term outlook. Both types are equally valid on a Personal Board.

Gender

In my experience, all genders have different outlooks, perspectives and ideas to execute a plan. With different levels of objectivity, risk aversion/mitigation, optimism and confidence, the sum of all the parts really does equal the whole.

Hearing both perspectives is invaluable – it prevents you from becoming your own echo chamber and only listening to the views that chime with your own. After all, the world is made up of a wide range of people, and to influence and lead others, you need to reflect all those views, not just your own.

Age/seniority

As mentioned in the section on reverse mentoring in Chapter 2, it's important to take counsel from different age groups, not just from your peers or seniors. It was traditionally the case that you'd only ask older and more senior people for advice. Most organisations were made up of hierarchies, and it was perceived that elders always knew best. That's not necessarily so these days.

Many industries – technology, my industry, being a prime example – are flatter in terms of structure, younger in terms of management profile, and faster moving in terms of lifecycle, meaning that the input of the younger generation is now much more important. Factor in the obvious social media influences and connection with the world in general, and the question should be: 'Why *aren't* you using younger people as a sounding board?'

When you talk to people younger than you, they will usually question your foundations, asking, 'How have you got to this point?' I always find this question invaluable, as it grounds me and allows me to check that I haven't gone off track. Think about it this way: In the corporate world, why would you have all fifty-year-olds on the board of a company such as Instagram if the audience demographic is made up of people in their twenties?

Social media has broken down barriers. Younger generations are now more comfortable providing opinions to more senior people, and often with a credible voice. This fluidity is fantastic for Personal Boards, enabling them to be more inclusive and encompass a wider range of opinions from different sources.

Thought: Neurodiversity

Many psychometric methodologies can help you consider the issue of diversity of thought. Cognitive diversity drives the inclusion of many different working styles and problem-solving abilities, which can provide unique perspectives on any given situation.

> **BACKGROUND INFORMATION: Cognitively diverse teams solve problems faster**
>
> In March 2017 *Harvard Business Review* featured an article, 'Teams Solve Problems Faster When They're More Cognitively Diverse', on why teams with greater cognitive diversity will usually achieve better results than those without.
>
> While it would be easy to think that other diversity factors previously discussed, such as background and education, might provide enough diversity, these markers are not necessarily predictors of different ways of thinking.

The same article explained how the AEM (attachment, exploration and managing) tool developed by Peter Robertson, a psychiatrist and consultant, assesses ways that individuals process information and what they consider should be the next steps.

It is unlikely you will be asking Personal Board members to take a test before you judge their suitability, but considering your Personal Board members in terms of how they think is a great check and balance.

Has anyone surprised you in the past with their creativity and ideas?

Perhaps they considered options you had not considered?

Or, when you asked people for advice, did they only put forward the ideas you'd already come up with?

You can pick your poison on this topic in terms of personality tests such as Myers Briggs or DISC (dominance, influence, steadiness, conscientiousness). However, rather than analysing people's profiles in detail, consider this simple point on the differences between introverts and extroverts:

Extroverts will speak their thoughts and talk about their views openly. Introverts will process everything internally first, weighing up the pros and cons before saying anything. Both approaches are equally valid.

Whichever one you prefer on your Personal Board will depend on your personality type, but as with everything, I'd recommend a mix – both approaches have strengths and weaknesses.

Multiple roles win the day

The final area to consider when assembling your list of needs is the role each person plays on your Personal Board. Let's think of this in relation to some of the roles that could feature on your board.

Partner

Your partner features as an individual role on your Personal Board. While they may have experience in your field of work, it is their knowledge and familiarity with your personal experiences and future goals that places them in a unique position to help you on your journey, if you would like them to feature on your board.

Friend

Similar to a partner, friends know your background and the context of where you have been and where you would like to go. Again, diversity is key, and having your entire friendship circle on your board is unlikely to fulfil the diversity objective. Therefore, consider retaining only one or two friends who have relevant experience that could help with your immediate goals.

Coach

Coaches are invaluable on a Personal Board. A coach is someone who helps you find your best and play at your best. They achieve this by asking questions and exploring ideas with you, on a journey of self-realisation, without giving you the answers.

A coach could be either a paid executive or somebody who has had leadership or coaching training and who you can ask to play this role on a pro bono basis.

Mentor

In contrast to a coach (who helps with self-reflection), mentors help by sharing their experience, knowledge and decision-making capabilities to provide options for different scenarios. Mentors are usually experienced people in an organisation or industry who can impart their relevant experience. They have been there and 'walked the walk'.

I previously mentioned reverse mentoring, which you could also consider for your board. In short: This is typically where you are more senior than your mentor but where their fresh perspective can provide insights without the 'baggage' associated with time and experience. Reverse mentoring can often unpick the status quo and illustrate less obvious paths.

Sponsor

Sponsors are those who are looking to help you get to your goals by providing their approval or recommendation. Champions of your cause, sponsors will publicly put themselves out there to promote your cause for you.

In-industry peer

In-industry peers can be useful, as they will be familiar with your personal brand and the landscape associated with getting to most of your desired goals, such as promotions, pay rises, start-up funding and CEO initiatives.

People often ask about recruiting more peers, but there are some potential drawbacks:

- **Competition:** They are likely to be going for the same jobs.
- **Chinese whispers:** You need a safe place to speak.
- **Numbers:** There are only so many internal peers you can confide in.

I have also learned a lot from my in-industry peers *because* they tend to be pushing for the same types of jobs so are at a similar level of knowledge and experience.

One to two from each of these categories would be a good number to add to your Personal Board. Too many of any category, and you will create risk by reducing diversity.

MY STORY: A peer group for life

The pros of peers

After I left BMC, I had the honour of being asked to continue to mentor several salespeople I had collected along my journey. They were good individual contributors who were great at their jobs, and they also wanted to grow into leadership roles.

I had learned a couple of big life skills being a leader at BMC, which I felt I needed to impart:

1. **Your network is vital in leadership**

   Forget any sycophantic reasons for assembling a network. The number-one job of any leader is the recruitment of great talent. It's a basic principle of leadership – the better your network, the easier it is to hire faster and more consistently, and with success through referencing.

2. **You need a safe environment**

   Leadership isn't easy, whatever the company. There are always trials, tribulations and difficult decisions that need to be made. You need someone who is on that journey with you, to be able to share those concerns and chew the fat in a safe environment.

With all this in mind, I introduced my mentees to each other. They were from different companies but all at the same level, with similar ambitions and values.

At the time of writing, they have all been friends with each other for around five years. They have gone from individual contributors to leaders, and all of them have moved companies since we first started mentoring.

When I catch up with them, I often ask how they are using each other as sounding boards. Here are some of their responses:

- Advice on managing the team
- Sharing ideas on best practices
- Knowledge of the industry
- Typical salary packages – their own and for their hires
- Finding great candidates

My advice to anyone, at any stage of their career, is to seek out or create a peer group like this. As you grow, your peers will also be growing, and they will be able to provide invaluable support as you move through the stages of your journey.

Your Personal Board should evolve with your career. Take some people along with you on your journey.

A healthy mix of internal and external peers is a real advantage. There is a downside: You must work hard to seek out the right external people, but it's worth it.

Out-of-industry peers

Out-of-industry peers have been some of my most interesting Personal Board additions over the years. These are people who know the role and the problem, and a little about you. They are often easy to access through your existing network. However, they are far enough removed from your exact issues, goals and challenges that they can provide a fresh perspective and informed counsel.

EXERCISE: Your current Personal Board review

Make some notes on the following points:

- As in previous sections, think first about your current organic board members – what sort of role are they playing today?
- Is there diversity in the roles these existing members are playing?
- What skills or experience are missing from these existing members today?

Consolidate and prioritise needs

Now you have a more detailed view of the gaps in your Personal Board, you can list the types of people you are looking for in greater detail, identifying them based on:

- Your goals
- Your existing board members
- The skills you need to access in the future
- The diversity of the team you have and the gaps you need to fill
- The roles you need people to play

Now you can start to get some names in the frame of people you want to approach to assemble your Personal Board.

Chapter review

This chapter described ways you can start building and assembling your Personal Board by identifying what is needed and who to approach.

Key takeaways

- Once you've decided on your goals, you need to identify the people who can help you reach them. As your goals change over time, so will your needs and your Personal Board members.

- A brief gap analysis exercise will allow you to pinpoint what you need for your Personal Board.

- Multiple roles win the day. The wider variety of people you have on your Personal Board, the broader scope of advice, new perspectives and help you will receive.

EXERCISE: Expanding your Personal Board

Take a moment to further summarise your Personal Board today:

- What are your personal goals and needs?
- Who is at your table today?
- What diversity exists? What is missing?
- What help could really accelerate progress?
- Who in your network could help you access this?

7
Finalising Your Personal Board

Finalising your Personal Board entails putting names in the frame, deciding who to go with, determining which subjects to discuss, and creating a regular cadence of working together.

Remember: A Personal Board is fluid. As your priorities change and your situations evolve, don't be afraid to connect with new people. That said, Personal Boards do benefit from a degree of stability. Like everything in life, it's all about balance.

For this chapter, then, let's focus on the final steps of preparation, covering:

- Assembling your board
- Expanding your horizons

- Getting names in the frame
- Identifying your first agendas

Assembling your Board

This is the meat of the conversation and where you get to pull together those amazing ideas and people to create the best board for you.

Working your gap list

Building your Personal Board is an iterative process. You will need to revisit the lists you previously created and bring all those ideas together into a working list.

Consider:

1. Your goals and gaps
   - What are your goals?
   - What types of people do you need to help you on your way?
2. Your organic board members
   - Who is already by your side?
   - What can they offer to your strategy?

3. Diversity of the team

   - What do you already have in terms of diversity?

   - What is still missing from the team you've assembled?

Once you have this recap, you'll be ready to create your list of targets.

Brainstorm the 1 + 1 = 3

Your immediate network is very useful and shouldn't be dismissed, but by expanding your thinking to connections that are one or two people removed from you, you can dramatically increase the talent pool and options available to you.

You may be thinking, 'How on earth do I pick people I don't already know for my Personal Board?' You can easily overcome this challenge with two simple approaches, as follows.

Online information

Information about people in your industry or those with certain skill sets is readily available today. LinkedIn, Twitter, TikTok and other memberships and social media platforms, all provide fantastic information on people you don't yet know.

Earlier on, you started to brainstorm the types of people you might want to know. With a few simple online searches, you can easily connect with a more diverse group.

MY STORY: Cornish angels

A leap of faith

In 2020, during the pandemic – after I'd lived in the most land-locked part of the country for all my life – the coast called.

I had always wanted one day to live on the coast and, with the on–off lockdowns now a part of everyday life, it seemed an obvious time to make the move. In September 2020 my family and I relocated to Penzance.

I had spent my entire working life travelling, so the commute to London or other cities for company and customer visits wasn't an issue for me. I actually enjoyed the focused time on the commute.

However, in the summer of 2022, I was spending more time working for myself and continuing to invest in start-ups through angel investing. I felt there was a real gap when it came to investing in Cornish businesses rather than defaulting to London-based companies, as I always had.

A cup of tea in hand, I sat and brainstormed how I could connect with businesses in Cornwall, either to angel invest in them or to help them grow through coaching and mentoring.

I needed some connections so I googled 'angel investing Cornwall'. The search results brought up Ralph, a speaker at an event for the UK Business

Angels Association. Ralph worked for a Truro-based organisation helping Cornish businesses to access funds and grants.

Again, as simple as it seems, I reached out on LinkedIn to Ralph with this message:

'Hi Ralph, I'm an angel investor, screener and advisor to Angel Academe, recently moved from London to Cornwall. Keen to get involved in the local start-up scene and saw your name on one of the UKBAA (UK Business Angels Association) events pages. Wondering if you would connect or perhaps signpost me to local angel/ venture capital communities to get involved. Thanks.'

As I'm writing this, I feel the need to confess that imposter syndrome kicked in – I didn't expect Ralph to respond, let alone meet with me. However, Ralph soon replied and we met face-to-face. Now I have not only started to build angel connections in Cornwall, but I have also linked up with local people who have children of similar ages to my own – an unexpected bonus in knowledge and connections.

When building your Personal Board to extend your network, it's important to have faith that humans want to help other humans.

Expanding your horizons

Your connections' connections

Even if you don't fancy a cold reach-out, the world is a small place, and your existing connections could easily help you extend your network reach.

Do an online search and you'll see that many sources suggest that the average person meets between 30,000 and 80,000 people throughout their life, and the advent of apps such as LinkedIn has encouraged us to consider not only our immediate (first-level) connections but also the connections of those people (second-level connections), and *their* connections, and so on.

BACKGROUND INFORMATION: Six degrees of separation

The six degrees of separation theory was attributed to the Hungarian author Karinthy Frigyes, who published a collection of short stories in 1929, one of which was entitled 'Chain-Links'. This argued that, despite greater physical distances between individuals, the growing density of human networks made the actual social distance far smaller.

An article in the *New Zealand Herald* tells the story of a spin-off theory which became known as The Six Degrees of Kevin Bacon – a game created by US students to see who could connect any actor with Kevin Bacon in the fewest hops. Bacon's Law claims that any actor is within six degrees of separation from Kevin Bacon.

When social media is coupled with globalisation, the degrees of separation (or hops) you need to reach someone have continued to reduce. Research has shown that by 2016 the average degrees of separation to reach anyone in the

---

world averaged 4.57, and by 2022, further research suggested that active social media users could connect to most people in around 3.6 connections.

With a few carefully placed requests for connections, the whole world becomes an abundant talent pool ready for you to access.

With three to four hops now to anybody out there, you have the entire world to call on to add the best, brightest and most useful connections to your Personal Board. Take this book, for example. In 2020, when I set the goal to write this, I didn't know anyone who had ever written a book. Within twenty-four hours of the goal being set, I had already had two conversations:

1. I held a Personal Board networking event. I said I was interested in writing a book and asked if anyone knew an author. Elaine at Salesforce connected me with the fabulous Alison, best-selling author of *Secrets of Successful Sales*, for Alison to then connect me to Mindy at Rethink Press Limited. Two hops and I had a publisher.

2. I mentioned to Karen at a networking event that I was planning to write a book. Karen kindly introduced me to Matt, a ghost writer, who helped me structure my thoughts and write the book with me. Just one hop and I had an experienced writer helping me – one of the fastest outcomes I have ever had from my network.

Most humans want to help. By sharing a little about yourself and your goals, your network can present you with amazing opportunities. While your existing network can help, use your imagination to create the best target list of contacts possible.

EXERCISE: Your VIP list

- Imagine if you could choose from anyone in the world to help you.

  Who would you choose and why?

- Focus on the gaps, needs, skills and goals you have collected so far.

  Who are the most important connections on your list of potential board members?

- Create your VIP list.

  Before you complete the list, give your existing board members a quick call to explore who else is available in their networks. Who can they think of?

Getting names in the frame

You should now be able to write down some names of people you would like to add to your Personal Board. The list will not be perfect. You may still have gaps, where over time you will ask your network to connect you to other people. However, you should have enough to make a start.

BACKGROUND INFORMATION: *Eat That Frog!* by Brian Tracy

You can plan as much as you like. However, in the long run, you will gain the most benefit by writing down a list of actions, committing yourself to those actions and starting to engage with people to recruit the connections you need.

If you are not the most confident of networkers, or if you suffer from imposter syndrome, asking people for their help or advice is probably a scary prospect, but you will soon gain confidence.

As I have mentioned previously, your goals will become more real when you verbalise them to others. While you can plan and plan and plan, ultimately you must work with others to commit yourself to those plans, especially if you are pushing yourself out of your comfort zone.

My advice: eat that frog.

One of my favourite books is *Eat That Frog!* by Brian Tracy. The book contains many great gems of advice. However, one has always stuck with me: To feel like you are making progress and get yourself on a roll, look at your to-do list. From that list, pick the ugliest, hairiest, dirtiest frog – the list item you have been procrastinating over or avoiding. Swallow this frog early in the morning – do something you don't want to do before choosing any of the other, nicer actions. You will then feel proud, relieved, exhilarated, and all the positive emotions in between.

The same applies to reaching out to your potential Personal Board members. Once you understand who you need and what you need, start making those connections and having those conversations that will propel you faster to your goals. Even if you have been dreading making that move, as soon as you start to gain valuable connections, the feeling of achievement will far outweigh any initial discomfort you were feeling.

Identifying your first agendas

You have your list of needs and your ideal list of prospects. Now you can hit the phone calls and emails required to start setting up those meetings. What will you say?

To get the help you need, from your target list of connections, you must now be specific about the help you are looking for. Time is precious for everyone, so you need to be sensitive in maximising the use of your Personal Board. Here is my best-practice advice for those first connections:

1. **Have a focused agenda**

   Make notes on what you need from your first session with this Personal Board member.

   Be specific about your goals and not too ambitious about the conversation outcome.

Good examples would be:

- Connect to **share** and **get feedback** on your two-year goals

- **Share** a challenge with a missing skillset and **brainstorm** possible help options

- **Ask for advice** on a promotion or interview process

- **Share** a business plan for a new or existing business and **get feedback** on gaps

2. **Be time-conscious**

Work out the minimum amount of time you need for your agenda. Time is precious to everybody. Remember you are asking for a favour, so you need to ensure you are not asking for too much from your contact.

I feel that twenty to thirty minutes is usually sufficient. Once you get into a rhythm with your contacts, it becomes easier to estimate the time needed.

Remember: You are asking for help, not looking to chew the fat – short and punchy meetings are best to make progress. Taking up a minimum amount of your board member's time will also make them happier to provide advice in the future.

3. **Plan meetings carefully**

Some of these contacts will be among the best in the industry, and more travel time equals less time spent with you. If meeting requests can be accommodated easily with minimal disruption, it's much more likely that people will agree to them. My advice is therefore that you go to them. Meet them at their offices, or when they're out and about, to limit the disruption to their day-to-day working life.

Remember: You want to maximise the amount of time they spend on discussing your career and goals rather than on travelling to and from meetings.

Chapter review

You should now be more comfortable with the concept of looking outside of your immediate circle for contacts for your Personal Board.

Key takeaways

- The first step is always the hardest, so remember to eat that frog. Prioritise securing external contacts before allowing yourself some easier tasks such as agenda setting.

- Remember: The more specifically you can articulate what you're looking for, the better.

- Make it as easy as possible for anybody you approach to agree to meetings. Be brief, and don't be vague.

EXERCISE: Eat that 'VIP' frog

Once you've resolved to take action, don't wait for a planning meeting or a free evening or weekend.

Scribble your thoughts down immediately on whatever is to hand, and try to think of who might be able to help you. I wrote my original concept for a Personal Board on a sheet of scrap paper at the kitchen table.

You don't necessarily need specific names. It could be that you decide you need to contact somebody in a certain position and need to research this further beforehand but, with your initial notes, you now have a starting point.

8
Using Your Board:
Part I – Personal Goals

The next two chapters contain detailed examples of how to use a Personal Board. Not all will apply, however, these examples can get anyone started on their journey. This first set of scenarios aims to provide the foundations for your development.

The planning process is critical to any endeavour you undertake. It just so happens that in this case, the endeavour is you, or You Inc.

It is important to think of yourself in the third person – as You Inc. – because you need to be able to look at yourself dispassionately, to see yourself as others see you. Only then can you start to objectively recognise your strengths and improve on your weaknesses.

The three-word feedback technique first mentioned in Chapter 2 comes in handy here.

At the beginning of this book, I talked about the importance of extending your network beyond your comfort group, ie, your friends and family. This is to access advice that is not only dispassionate but also informed – people who know what they are talking about for a specific situation, industry, job type, etc.

With this in mind, let's look at ways of thinking laterally, to broaden your network early on in your career beyond your normal comfort groups, with examples of peer-to-peer and junior boards.

Scenario 1: Formalise your goals

I have emphasised the need to have an agenda for your Personal Board meetings. However, it's perfectly OK to use these meetings to brainstorm ideas to create goals; just remember to make this clear on the agenda. In Chapter 5, I outlined how you could start to put some goals together. It is often helpful to go through this goal-setting process with somebody else, to help the planning process come alive, so this could also be the purpose of a Personal Board meeting.

Let's think about how you can structure these conversations with your Personal Board members.

Sample agenda

- Introductions (if needed)
- Background to your career history
- Goal-setting process
  - Brainstorm your future state and personal ambitions
  - Identify your passions and happiest days
  - Identify possible paths
  - Identify the next steps needed to qualify or move forward
- Commit to your three next steps, based on today's conversation
- Any other business (AOB)

To commit to your next three steps – the penultimate point above – you will need to reflect and create the actions for yourself. Remember: The best corporate boards are those that guide and advise. They are not there to create these actions or complete them for you. If the actions are not yours, you simply will not commit to them.

The agenda above will give you a great start to validating some goals. You could repeat this with multiple members to gain different perspectives and ideas, which will help you in crystallising your goals.

Scenario 2: Brand review

Our goals, ambitions and dreams usually depend on other people, and the decisions that those people make will have far-reaching effects on our lives. Therefore, it is imperative to understand what people think of you now, and how you need them to think of you going forward, so you can plug any gaps to ensure the two perceptions are aligned.

Your brand is the reputation that precedes you and how people perceive you. With people you haven't met before, your reputation might be based largely on first impressions. Therefore, as you wander into new territory, your brand must match your goals as closely as possible.

Personal brand review – Step 1: Solicit feedback

Three-word feedback

The phrase 'personal feedback' brings many people – at any level of seniority or experience – out in a cold sweat. In my experience, the main reasons people shy away from soliciting personal feedback are as follows:

- **Fear:** People rarely welcome honest feedback, worrying about what they might hear about themselves and what might reinforce their inner critic.

- **Negative bias:** The chances are, even if somebody receives lots of positive feedback and one piece of constructive feedback, they will discount the positives and focus exclusively on the implied negative.

- **Perplexity:** How do you ensure you receive the feedback in a digestible format that you can do something with?

Unstructured feedback can therefore do more harm than good, sending your inner critic into overdrive so the only words you remember are the negative ones.

Here's how I recommend soliciting personal feedback:

1. Write down three words that you think represent yourself.

2. Ask your Personal Board member to write down three words that they think reflect you.

3. Compare, contrast and discuss the two lists.

Your own three words could all be positive ones. This isn't a bad way to start, as it makes the personal feedback exercise a confidence booster. Then you could introduce, or ask for, just one improvement word. This has the benefit of limiting negative feedback – the fuel for your inner critic.

This three-word method is a spin on Carla Harris's methodology, as explained in her best-selling series of books.

BACKGROUND INFORMATION: *Expect to Win and Strategize to Win* **by Carla Harris**

Understand your brand

Carla Harris is an incredibly smart, academic lady, who was a banker at Morgan Stanley for over thirty years. When she started her career, Carla thought that hard work and determination alone would be enough to achieve her goals. That was until she realised that people considered her to be:

- More important than her own perception
- Not necessarily the same as her perception of herself

Carla stresses how important it is to understand what your brand means to other people, and then to ensure that their perception matches what you need it to be. To achieve this, you need:

- **Feedback** – and plenty of it – to understand their perceptions
- **To ask open questions** and be curious about their feedback

Armed with this foundational information, you can then adapt your language and behaviours to influence your personal brand, to help others see you how they need to see you.

I highly recommend watching Carla Harris on YouTube and also reading her books, *Expect to Win* and *Strategize to Win*.

There are other advantages to the three-word feed-back method. They are:

- **Confidence-boosting:** Often, your Personal Board member will think of positive words about you that you hadn't thought of. This gives you insight into how others value you and provides you with more positives to focus on.

- **Safely presented:** Because you've set the agenda and the scope of the feedback, there is no danger of this turning into a 'hatchet job', ie, a fierce attack on you or your work. You will receive bite-sized feedback, which you can digest in a safe environment.

- **Actionable:** You can do something with this feedback. If your Personal Board member's positive words match your own, that's great. However, if they don't, you can explore why this might be and take steps to make your self-perception others' perceptions of you. This might only require you to reinforce a particular quality in other people's minds.

AYLSA'S STORY: Three-word feedback with rejection

Seek out the scary feedback

I met Aylsa five years ago when we worked at the same company and often found ourselves at similar coaching events, both of us trying to learn more about helping others grow.

Earlier this year, Aylsa reached out to me for advice. She had been looking for a promotion and had applied for several positions. Unfortunately, with every position she applied for, she found herself pipped at the post.

Aylsa told me about her experiences and about how she couldn't understand how she could make a difference to land the next big role. I asked casually about the feedback the hiring managers had given for not choosing Aylsa as their first choice. Unsurprisingly, though – like so many of these situations – the hiring teams had not provided feedback, and Aylsa had not pushed the point.

I asked why she had not asked for feedback, and Aylsa admitted she had been fearful of the answer. As soon as these words passed her lips, she knew what she needed to do.

Aylsa asked for a quick debrief with one of the hiring teams. I had suggested using the three-word technique to make the feedback more manageable.

The feedback? Aylsa had appeared outgoing, task-orientated and customer-focused, but the brief for the role had focused on strategy, strategy and strategy. By Aylsa's own admission, she hadn't even considered the role's description and hence hadn't pitched for the role in a way that conveyed strategy at the core of her competencies.

A simple chat with her Personal Board before an interview could have identified three keywords, which Aylsa could have checked against the job role. In a future interview, this is exactly what she did. And guess what? She landed the role.

Feedback can be scary. Use the three-word technique to gather feedback and to consider what you need to land that next step on your career path.

Personal brand review – Step 2: Who needs to care?

Why do you want feedback? It could be to:

- **'Sharpen the axe':** As in the saying made famous by Abraham Lincoln, before you set to the task, work on your self-awareness.

- **Drown out your inner critic:** Your inner critic is often the loudest voice in your head and needs to be kept in check. Positive feedback is always confidence-boosting if you allow yourself to listen to it.

- **Understand yourself better:** Find out what others think you're great at, or (with constructive criticism) where could you 'sharpen your axe'?

- **Influence others:** One of the best reasons for soliciting feedback is to ensure the people who make decisions about your career or business are aligned with how you want and need to be perceived. This will increase your level of influence over them and your career path.

- **Prepare for the next process:** Promotions and pay rises are influenced by other people.

THE PERSONAL BOARD OF YOU INC.

Understanding how they perceive you, and if the feedback is not as you would like it to be, will enable you to create an action plan.

Personal brand review – Step 3: Make your feedback actionable

Now you have a few sets of words:

- The words you want to be known for

- The words you have solicited in feedback

- The words you need to be known for to progress

If all words match, great – you know you're pitching yourself along the right lines. One of the key strengths of a Personal Board is that it provides a range of feedback, so do check your three-word list with feedback from your other Personal Board members for a fuller picture.

If your sets of three words *don't* match, you can:

- **Brainstorm with your Personal Board:** If one or all of your keywords are critical, consider the actions you could take to ensure external perceptions match up.

- **Change your perception or words:** Having checked with a couple of Personal Board

USING YOUR BOARD: PART I - PERSONAL GOALS

members first, if the external perception of you is consistent, then focus on the positives – look at yourself in a new light and see where the new path might lead you.

- **Consider actions to course correct:** Consider the actions you can take with your Personal Board to change the perception of others. Do you need to modify your actions, your references or the language that you use?

You can play around with this concept. For example, you could brainstorm with your Personal Board and ask them to identify three keywords that represent the attributes a great sales manager (or whatever position you are targeting) should possess and then work towards these three attributes.

In short: *Three words can become your personal brand roadmap.* **They help you to understand where you are now and where you're heading.**

Scenario 3: Building for the future

If I could give my twenty-year-old self any advice, it would be to focus early on expanding my network. While I have always had some focus on my network, I'd say I have only recently realised how valuable it is, and how much more valuable it could have been had I pushed those connections earlier on in my career. There is a balance, though. I have never believed in being a LION (LinkedIn open networker), where you randomly connect to anyone without any rhyme or reason.

You do need to exhibit some emotional intelligence in asking people for connections – don't ask for too much too quickly. That said, for those twenty-somethings out there (and for people even younger): starting to extend your network early can provide a wide range of opportunities, such as:

- Future job opportunities

- Peer-to-peer support

- Upskilling opportunities

- Raising your professional profile

You'll find some examples here of ideas for how you might use your Personal Board in the earlier stages of your journey.

Preparing for a change in the composition of your Personal Board

As you move through life, your roles will change, and the composition of your Personal Board will also need to adapt accordingly.

I used to coach and mentor a group of young, ambitious salespeople, who all wanted to step up and become leaders, having been promoted to their first management jobs. It soon became clear that these group members all had the same questions:

- How do I prepare for the interview?

- How do I demonstrate leadership qualities?

- How do I create a 90-day plan – the key activities and accomplishments I need to achieve in my first 90 days?

- How will I hire and lead?

This got me thinking about:

1. How could they share experiences to 'self-support' going forward?

2. How would I help them connect to create a support network for the future?

One of the best ways to get ready for these questions is to create a good peer network, which includes people who are ambitiously chasing the same path as you. It's likely that, as you start to step up and make your career moves, others in your peer network will be making similar moves. You then have a pre-built peer group, which can support you through your career.

MY STORY: The lifelong peer group

'It takes a village to raise a child.' – African proverb

In 2018 I was mentoring four interesting salespeople, all of whom had ambitions to go on to become sales managers. I was struck by the similarities in their career progressions and personal goals, so I suggested they would do well to connect. My thinking was that, although they were working in different organisations, they were all peers in the same industry. Therefore, as they grew into leadership roles, they would be able to provide peer support to each other.

That's exactly what happened. All four are now leaders in the tech industry, and they continue to cooperate regularly, connecting for the following reasons:

- **Peer-to-peer mentoring:** Discussing everyday challenges
- **Recruitment connections:** Helping each other to recruit
- **Connections for new roles themselves:** A couple of them even worked together now in the same company

The forum for Personal Board meetings can be one-to-one or one-to-few. One-to-few meetings are useful when you meet with peers who are on the same journey, enabling the sharing of advice and support.

Junior boards

It is important to stress that Personal Boards are not only for senior people. In fact, quite the opposite – as with pensions, it's best to start them young. Juniors (a term used here only to distinguish people relatively new to the workplace from more senior/ tenured people) will benefit from starting early in taking control of their careers, and learning how to plan, organise and develop their skill sets and working lives.

A huge leap of faith is required if you are at the outset of your career. It is common, when embarking on a new journey, not to know exactly where you are headed. This lack of clarity and confidence can easily result in a fear that you will be messing people around if you ask them for their time and connections.

While I do not recommend that you waste people's time, I can guarantee that if you are polite, courteous and considerate in your approach, you will grow a network that will become invaluable later in life. Again, based on the now, remember the three degrees of separation.

Here is an example of a short agenda, which you could use with new connections and with new Personal

Board members, to help inspire ideas for your potential future agenda:

- Ask your Personal Board member about their story.

- What is the biggest challenge they have faced and how did they overcome it?

- Who has had the biggest influence on their career and why?

- Where are they headed? What are their goals? How have these goals changed over the years?

For juniors, Personal Boards provide invaluable experience, support and mentoring, and connections that will be useful down the line. The relationships you build today and how you use that advice and guidance early on in your career will provide you with more choices for the future.

Chapter review

The change starts with you. It may sound trite if I say you need to understand yourself first, but you need to be crystal-clear about yourself and your needs when communicating with somebody who might not yet know you well.

Although the idea of reaching out to ask for career help might sound slightly scary, think of it as a chance to reposition yourself. Your organic contacts already know you well, so you don't need to articulate yourself to them, but that can be a disadvantage as their image of you is rearward-looking (the person they knew) rather than forward-looking (the person you wish to be).

Key takeaways

- To be clear on what you want, you first need to be clear about who you are; ie, you need to understand your brand.

- Techniques such as the three-word feedback are great for constructive feedback, both in confidence-boosting and in providing you with areas for improvement and food for thought. Remember to check out Carla Harris on this point.

- Never underestimate the power of feedback – seek it out wherever and whenever possible.

EXERCISE: Lateral thinking

Make notes on where you might be able to access feedback about yourself. It could be from people senior to you or junior to you.

If you happen to know people at similar stages of their careers, you could access feedback from your peer group, as in the real-life story 'The lifelong peer group' in this chapter.

9
Using Your Board:
Part II – Career Goals

In this second set of scenarios, I'll cover a variety of career applications for your Personal Board, from starting out, to moving up the career ladder, right through to senior executive level. The concept remains the same throughout your career, so you don't have to reinvent the wheel as you progress. However, in the modern world, it's not just about having a single career or a job for life – those days are long gone.

You will need to build (and rebuild) your networks over time, for example when you decide to set up your own business or have a portfolio career of part-time roles, or if you intend to seek out directorships once you've made it to senior executive level

The sooner you can get comfortable with the concept of a Personal Board, the sooner you'll be able to flex this to your advantage in line with your chosen career path.

Scenario 1: Any new role or skills

Your Personal Board is a diverse group of people with a broad set of skills and experiences. It can help you when you are transitioning into a new role or new industry, or even a new phase in your life such as returning to work from maternity leave.

A sample agenda for a regular check-in with a Personal Board member could look something like this:

- Provide an update on your current situation.

- Discuss the challenges in your transition.

  - What are you experiencing?

  - What are you expecting to experience?

- Talk about the help and support you may need during that transition.

  - Is frequent contact for regular support required?

- Agree actions before the next meeting.

When you take on a new role or return from a break, it's easy to get wrapped up in the busyness of work and struggle to make time for reflection and thinking.

However, in a transition period, this time is needed more than ever, to make sense of your new challenges and to ensure you stay on the right track for your journey.

> **BACKGROUND INFORMATION: *Time to Think* by Nancy Kline**
>
> In *Time to Think*, Nancy Kline describes how the quality of your attention will define the quality of someone else's thinking.
>
> The book focuses on the power of effective listening and the art of asking insightful questions. This is exactly what you want from your Personal Board members – the ability to listen to your issues and, by doing so, to clarify your thinking.
>
> The inspiration for Nancy's book was her mother, who, while an ordinary person, was an extraordinary listener. The author encourages this fine art of listening, including not interrupting, not seeking to promote one's thoughts, and always laughing with someone and never at them.
>
> **Our Personal Boards can be there to listen and help you decipher your thoughts through difficult times and complex scenarios.**

Scenario 2: Extending your network

Your network is the keystone – the foundation – of your Personal Board strategy. As we've already discussed, a Personal Board should not be a static concept. It needs to evolve alongside you, adapting to your career, your promotions, new markets, new sectors, new skills, etc.

Common stumbling blocks to extending your network include:

- 'I just don't know how to get those connections.'
- 'I don't know how to meet the people I need for my Personal Board.'
- 'I'm not comfortable searching for people I don't already know.'

Today's generation has a significant advantage when setting up a Personal Board. The internet and the advent of social media render the world a far smaller, more intimate space, as evidenced by the original six degrees of separation theory having been reduced, by 2016, to less than four degrees.

If you have any reservations about extending your network, remember the specific purposes for and benefits of your Personal Board:

- **New role**

  - Acquire new skills for the new elements of the role.

  - Increase your ideas and knowledge of a new industry.

  - Expand your network, getting to know key people in the industry.

- **Customer connections**

  - Extend your client base if you are starting a business.

  - Make customer connections if you are engaged in a customer-facing role.

- **New territory/country**

  - Improve your local market knowledge and connections.

- **Peer review**

  - Benefit from new peer-to-peer connections.

There are endless benefits to expanding your network. Pretty much any new role, business or promotion will require a shake-up and expansion of your network.

Here are some points on how you can specifically drive this agenda with your Personal Board and how to ask your board members to provide you with their valuable personal connections.

Asking contacts for contacts

It's simple. There are people out there who can potentially help you, but you don't know them. However, some of your network contacts do.

One of the most effective uses for your Personal Board is to brainstorm additional connections that could impact your situation or future.

MATT AND SHAUN'S STORY: Seeking out the right people to advise

Preparing for your environment

I had worked with Matt and Shaun at SAP some years before they left to start bigger roles at a different company.

On starting their new roles, they realised that the company was lacking hungry salespeople who knew how to hunt out new leads. This didn't match with the high-growth profile envisaged by the company and shareholders, so Matt and Shaun had a lot of work to do to drive a different culture and recruit new people.

To complicate matters further, the company had recently been acquired. Matt and Shaun therefore also needed to wrestle with the company's change in culture, while driving results and navigating a politically tricky situation with new owners and management.

They needed help. This was not an environment familiar to them.

They initially reached out to me, as I had worked for several high-growth companies and there was possibly a parallel.

However, the biggest help I could offer was with ideas on more suitable connections. After fifteen minutes of brainstorming the challenge, we identified three other contacts who had experienced and successfully navigated a similar scenario.

Matt and Shaun quickly reached out to those connections, and one offered to meet with them regularly to help in the early days to get them on the right road.

Use your Personal Board to brainstorm. Who else might be able to help you with your situation? Who else might your contacts be able to connect you with?

When asking your contacts for new connections, the trick is to make the introduction quick and easy. You then need to 'sell' the meeting and arrange it with as little hassle for the other person as possible.

If these are new connections and you are looking for a deeper level of help and assistance, there will be a process you will need to go through to establish the new link, to build the relationship and rapport, before finally asking the connection to help you. This does take time and should be a consideration when you are thinking about what you are going to ask of them.

PRACTICAL TIP: Quick introductions via LinkedIn

Linking with LinkedIn

The first two examples below are connection requests I have sent when someone has asked me for an introduction. The third example is an introduction I received via LinkedIn, proving that it does work both ways.

Example 1

Hi Lucy – thanks for connecting again. Introducing you to Tanya who is a founder of a company in which I'm invested, who is looking for a legal person three days a week-ish. I'll leave you both to connect. I think there could be a good match here.

Example 2

Gary, meet Mark. Recalling our conversation yesterday, I think you'd benefit from engaging Mark on some MEDDIC/value-based selling training to help grow your sales team. Worth a conversation. I'll leave you in Mark's capable hands.

Example 3

Emma, meet Rebecca; Rebecca, meet Emma!

Emma, Rebecca has a start-up in my world, and I thought you guys should meet.

Good luck!

Fred

These examples illustrate just how easy it is to make initial connections. There's no guarantee every person will respond positively to every request they receive, but I think you will be pleasantly surprised by nearly all the reactions you receive.

Linking people in this manner costs me virtually nothing in time, and providing I have thought carefully about a connection that will be relevant and useful, I have managed to help both parties. This way I am placing a penny in the jar for a later day when I might need a connection.

Most senior people understand the value of helping others, whether that is for building connections, enhancing their personal brand or simply for the good feeling from helping others. When I hear of an opportunity or receive a request, I immediately consider whether there is anybody in my network who might be able to help, and I'd say that around 80% of the time somebody gets something materially useful out of the situation. It's worked for me many times over with my Personal Board, and I am confident it will continue to yield results.

LARA'S STORY: Making entrepreneurial connections

A health check for Lara's business

Lara is the CEO and co-founder of a company called ImproveWell, which was founded to improve staff and patient experience.

I met Lara through Angel Academe, where she had successfully sought investment for what was at that time an early-stage business.

As the company started to grow, Lara began to get increasing interest from different NHS organisations, helping to accelerate her sales.

However, Lara felt something was missing in the advisors she had been collecting along the way. She had great angels and well-connected clinicians, but an NHS workforce specialist would be able to give real-life feedback on how and why different types of NHS organisations might invest in such a solution.

I had previously connected with Nicola, CEO of NHS Professionals, through another connection and felt that she could be a great match to help Lara.

Interestingly, when Nicola and I had first met, our direct universes had been different and we struggled to find something tangible to work on together. However, through Lara, this would become a great connection.

Lara and Nicola immediately hit it off, and Nicola subsequently joined ImproveWell's board as a chairperson, providing crucial, direct insight into how to drive improved patient care and well-being, both for professionals and patients.

Personal Boards can be vital sources of connections for entrepreneurs who are usually incredibly busy, short of time and often in a new market they did not expect to be in.

Scenario 3: Transitional support

I have talked about how Personal Boards can help you get to the next step on your journey, but what about after you have reached that next step? You will often need help and support to make a career move successful, and this is another point where Personal Board members can help.

Ideas for agendas for your Personal Board after you have made the transition:

- **Creating a 90-day plan**
    - What are the key activities and accomplishments you need to achieve in your first 90 days?
    - What help and support might you need to achieve those?
    - What are the risks and issues that you might face, and how you could mitigate them?
- **Instigating a feedback loop with stakeholders**
    - Who are the key stakeholders in your new role?
    - Have you discussed with them what they need from you in the first 90 days?
    - How will you work with them to give feedback and continue to communicate?

- **Balancing busy with productive**

  - Review your day-to-day activity to ensure you are not 'just getting busy'.

  - Brainstorm with your Personal Board the must-do versus the need-to-do activities.

  - How can you be surgical with your actions to build the right connections and feedback for the future, rather than meeting with everyone (which is impossible)?

- **Peer support**

  - Work with your peers for general support – the 'Is this normal?' questions.

  - Use your Personal Board to sense-check the activities and challenges you are working on.

Peers are invaluable for transitional support. This applies equally whether you are an entrepreneur, self-employed or a new manager, or if you have been appointed to a new role. The initial leap can be scary and the onboarding and transition into the role will require some support for a while. Use your Personal Board to help with this.

JULES'S STORY: Putting a support network in place

The lonely world of entrepreneurship

In Chapter 2, I told you about Jules, who had worked in the beauty industry for most of her working life. Then, during the pandemic, which had a significant impact on the hair and beauty industry, Jules decided she needed a career change.

Jules used the time during lockdown to reskill in marketing tools that helped companies with their B2C and B2B marketing, for their websites, social media and general enquiries.

In 2022, Jules launched her new business, Creativa, and couldn't have been happier or more excited.

There was only one problem. Jules had gone from a job and role where there was a steady stream of people to chat with – clients, colleagues, suppliers – to working on her own.

The silence was deafening, giving rise to a constant dialogue with her inner critic, which soon became difficult to endure. Jules reached out to a friend and quickly realised that the lack of social connection had become a problem. This was not something she had anticipated.

Jules needed to get her support network in place – people she could call on for a coffee or a chat, working with each other or simply co-working in a space, to fill the void and support her through the transition.

Your Personal Board can be a great source of support through a transition period. This can make up the agenda of your first meetings, as long as the Personal Board members are happy to provide you with support and connections.

Scenario 4: Promotions and new roles

One of the most obvious uses for a Personal Board is the preparation for a promotion or new role. As mentioned previously, we would love life to be a meritocracy, with everyone being appreciated and promoted according to merit. However, unfortunately, people are busy in their own worlds, which means you can often be overlooked if you don't have someone advocating for you. You may also assume that people know who you are and what you stand for when you apply for a new role or promotion, but that is sadly not always the case.

MILENA'S STORY: Getting the next role

Figure out what you want... and go out and get it

I briefly worked with Milena at SAP. Milena connected with me again recently as she had been hoping to achieve the next big challenge in her career. However, she had hit a wall.

We jumped on Zoom for a chat.

Milena had applied for three new roles but had been unsuccessful. She was perplexed – she felt she had the right experience, outlook, skills and capabilities for the roles, and yet... three rebuffs.

We spent time discussing the roles and experiences, and then I asked her some questions.

'Did you *want* the roles?'

Strange as it sounds, Milena quickly realised that she hadn't wanted two of the roles. On reflection, she had initially applied for some interview experience, after not having changed roles for a while. While those rejections were disappointing, they weren't a real setback for her career.

Most experienced interviewers, especially for senior roles, can smell indifference a mile off. A lack of ambition, commitment or desire for a role doesn't make for a dedicated employee, making it easy to decline them.

'Did you ask for feedback?'

Milena's answer again: 'No'.

As mentioned in Chapter 8, feedback is not something we solicit easily and often. After a rejection, we are even more afraid to ask for feedback, as we assume it will be negative.

Milena immediately sought feedback so she could understand where she performed well in the interview and where she needed to improve or demonstrate additional capabilities.

We now had a couple of areas for Milena to focus on:

- Roles that Milena wanted
- Using feedback to improve Milena's pitch

I heard from Milena a couple of weeks later:

> Hi Emma
>
> I wanted to come back to you following our meeting a few weeks ago.
>
> I cannot tell you enough what a profound impact our conversation had on me. Firstly, in the way I became obsessed with Carla Harris, listening to all her videos on YouTube and reading her book. I thank you so much for introducing me to this inspiring woman. It feels like I was craving inspiration and you offered it to me.
>
> Then, I consolidated my thoughts, sat down and prepared myself for a conversation with a company that had grabbed my attention at the time.
>
> I now have the offer in hand and am ready to accept. Thanks so much for the tips. Let's connect again soon,
>
> Milena

Personal Boards can offer the simplest of advice, often simply by providing a new perspective for the next promotion or role.

Using Milena's story as a template, here are some ideas on how to use your Personal Board to help you prepare for that next role.

Agenda 1: Create your strategy for the role

Your Personal Board can help in creating the strategy for getting the role you are hoping for.

Interview processes should be run like sales cycles. Thinking about some basic foundations of how you might run a sales cycle will help close *your* deal.

Schedule a session with a couple of your Personal Board members and work through this suggested list of questions:

- About the role
  - What is the role?
    - Have you qualified this as a good role for you?
  - What capabilities and experience are they looking for?
    - How does your experience relate to this?
  - How can you mitigate any risks in your background?
    - What are you missing from the capabilities list?
    - Do you have other skills / capabilities that may be relevant?

- What should your pitch include?

    - What makes you the best person for this position?

    - How can you highlight the right experience and capabilities?

- What questions do you have about the role?

    - Do you need to qualify anything, eg, their decision criteria?

- About the people

    - Who are the stakeholders in the interview process?

        - What are their hiring criteria? If you don't know, can you find out?

        - Are you connected with them?

        - How can you influence their decision?

- About the competition

    - How many people are likely to be in the process?

        - What is their background and capability?

        - Where are they in the process today?

All you are doing here is brainstorming the likely outcomes. Think about the interview process purposefully so you make the best of every engagement with a future employer, giving yourself the best chance of securing the role.

Once you have this mapped out, you can take action to prepare your pitch.

Agenda 2: Be pitch-ready

Preparation will make you less nervous. This might seem an obvious point, but many people do not prepare fully for interviews by practising their pitch beforehand and thinking about the questions the interviewers might pose.

Make sure you have a three-minute pitch ready to use at the beginning of the interview, which provides:

- An introduction about yourself
- Details on your background and experience
- Your key highlights and accomplishments
- How your previous successes will help in the new role
- Pitch conclusion – why you feel you are right for the role

You should also be prepared to address any obvious risks, including any capabilities you are missing, and have an action plan ready to address these.

Get your pitch together and then ask one or two Personal Board members to conduct a mock interview with you and listen to your pitch. Also, have your mock interviewers ask you questions so you can practise for those live moments.

If you have chosen your Personal Board well, with plenty of diversity, you will have some experienced managers who can provide you with good mock interviews and feedback ideas in the Q&A.

PRACTICAL TIP: Likely interview questions

James Reed is the chairman of Reed, the recruitment specialist. He has written a series of blogs on the most commonly asked interview questions, and how to tackle them. Here are the six most common questions:

- Tell me about yourself.
- What are your weaknesses?
- Why should you get this job?
- What are your salary expectations?
- Where do you see yourself in five years?
- Do you have any questions?

You'll find these and other potential questions, all with tips on how to answer them, on the Reed.co.uk website.

For a more complete run-down, James has also written a book, *Why You?: 101 interview questions you'll never fear again*.

The preface on Amazon sums it up nicely: 'From classic questions like "tell me about yourself" and "what are your greatest weaknesses?" to puzzlers like "sell me this pen" and "how many traffic lights are there in London?", James Reed reveals what interviewers are really asking.'

The introduction to the book is even more insightful, telling of a chance encounter that led to rock history. Guitarist Andy Summers tells of a chance encounter on a train with drummer Stewart Copeland, which led to the formation of the band, The Police. They struck up a conversation in which they told each other what sort of music they wanted to make, each convincing the other of their sincerity and suitability. They therefore joined forces, went on to recruit Sting, form The Police... and the rest is history. Andy Summers entitled his autobiography 'One Train Later', in memory of his sliding-doors moment when he met Stuart Copeland.

In a nutshell, that describes what happens at a good job interview – two people talking from the heart about a common interest, each setting out what they have to offer the other.

Don't let your interview become a 'What if?'

Personal Boards can ask you reflective questions to help you prepare for your next big move.

Agenda 3: Live updates to your pitch and plan

You have brainstormed the process, got your pitch together and perfected it. Now you are ready to go.

For most career changes, there will be multiple stages to complete, especially for the more senior roles. It's also likely there will be a gap between interviews, giving you time to refine your pitch and questions, and reflect with your Personal Board.

Here are a few examples of questions your Personal Board members could explore with you in between interview stages, to further develop your pitch:

- How did your pitch go?
  - Did it resonate with the interviewer?
- Did you gather any feedback?
  - Were any concerns or risks in your experience highlighted?
- Did you gather any decision criteria on how the process might go?
  - What are they looking for?
- Do you need to refine your pitch?
  - Can you focus on additional areas to demonstrate your capability?

- Is the process running as expected?

  - Are there any changes you might need to make to your campaign?

You can also use this feedback loop to start thinking about the future. Have you heard anything you may need to focus on if you are successful in this application? Do you have the skills to deal with the issues identified or will you need help (from your Personal Board)?

MY STORY: Never stop asking for feedback

Who are you backing?

When I applied to SAP Concur in 2017, I made it through to the first stages and was one of the final two interviewees for the role.

I had been working with Nikki, an executive coach and a good friend, who had been supporting me through the interview process and helping with live campaign coaching.

Delighted to hear I was down to the final two, I called Nikki to give her an update:

'Just to let you know: I met with Chris again today, and he confirmed I'm one of the final two candidates. Just one interview left now, with Chris's boss.'

While I was still rejoicing at my progress, Nikki immediately had more questions:

'Do you know who the other candidate is? Also, who is Chris recommending for the role? Ultimately, you will be working for him, so who does he want?'

I hadn't even considered the fact that I should determine Chris's preferred candidate and whether he might be trying to influence his boss's decision. Nikki and I discussed some additional questions and outlined what I needed to have in place for the final interview. I then composed myself, ready to give Chris a call.

To cut a long story short: I asked him for any additional feedback and gently enquired about his preferred candidate. Phew – it was me! I also asked him whether he would be confirming this to his boss, effectively sponsoring me, before the final interview. Phew – he said yes!

Soon after, I received a formal offer.

While interview processes do need to be confidential due to the often delicate nature of roles and company confidentiality, use your Personal Board as support for these important life-changing processes.

Senior executive – Safe environment

As you progress in your career, the need for a confidential space to reflect and gather your thoughts becomes even more critical.

Senior executives are involved in many transformational processes that require reflection time. To name just a few of these processes:

- People changes/organisational restructures
- Decisions about mergers and acquisitions
- Expansion or downsizing challenges
- Corporate financing

While normal, run-of-the-business issues can be discussed with your peers, I found that, as I became more senior and had more people under me, it was often difficult to discuss many subjects with those same peers due to conflicts of interest. Again, I was able to turn to my Personal Board for help.

My Personal Board provided a safe environment where I could discuss challenges, brainstorm strategies and plans and consider options and risks. In my senior roles, I frequently used my Personal Board for:

- **Executive coaching**

  The companies I worked for always provided an executive coach. This provided reflection time for me to consider the trickier issues I was facing.

  As the coaches were under the company NDA (non-disclosure agreement), I could disclose details of the challenges I was facing and think them through with a 'thinking partner'. This helped me organise my thoughts and decide on the next steps.

- **Mentors to validate ideas**

  Once the thinking wheels were in motion, I then turned to mentors – again in confidence – to solicit advice on the ideas and plans I was now considering. This allowed me to validate these plans with people who had similar backgrounds and experiences, and who could guide me through the journey.

When making tough personnel changes, a senior executive needs to consider all angles. People are diverse, therefore, to understand all perspectives, it's imperative to gather a diverse set of views before making key decisions. No one knows everything, that's why we all need support and guidance.

Chapter review

The scenarios in this chapter illustrate the flexibility of the Personal Board concept, and the personal stories are included to open your mind to the real-life potential of your own Personal Board.

You should now be aware that there is no single 'right' way to use a Personal Board. You can use it in whatever way works for you, your situation and your specific needs, while remembering and adhering to the guiding principles covered in Chapter 4. Trust and respect, regular engagement, and guidance and advice are crucial to the success of a Personal Board, and I recommend you refer back to Chapter 4 until those principles are second nature to you.

Key takeaways

- Your Personal Board can act as a support network for career transitions, which cannot be underestimated.

- Use your Personal Board to prepare for those transitions – they can validate your path and help you prepare for the key meetings / events.

- Personal Boards are hugely valuable for all levels of careers. Senior executives can benefit from the creation of a safe environment to grow.

EXERCISE: Who has helped/could help?

Review the last two chapters and select a couple of scenarios on how a Personal Board could help you.

- Use the questions to start to brainstorm specific asks of the board members.
- Consider your gaps – who/what is missing from your support group?
- How will you engage with your members? Who first? For what and how often?

10
Feedback And Sustaining Your Personal Board

This chapter is about how to provide feedback to your Personal Board and how to sustain the relationships with your all-important members.

Keeping your board up to date, engaged and ready to help is imperative for the journeys you will be taking with your career. It is unlikely that any conversations you have will ever be one-offs, without any follow-up required or the need to connect again. It's therefore important you nurture these relationships to keep those people engaged during your onward journey.

The importance of feedback for your board

If this book has resonated with you, by now you will be thinking about how you can access the best minds in the world to help you to achieve your goals and ambitions. You will also have realised how vital it is to receive feedback.

Feedback is just as important for the Personal Board member, to let them know that they are adding value.

PRACTICAL TIP: Altruism

The need for a feedback loop and regular contact

Why do people want to help others? Think about senior mentors in the industry – why do they keep giving up their time to help and assist others further down the ladder?

1. **Oxytocin Rush I:** When you ask for help, the other person receives an oxytocin rush from being asked for assistance.

2. **Oxytocin Rush II:** When some advice resonates and the mentee has a lightbulb moment, the mentor gets a second rush from seeing that they have helped in some way.

3. **Oxytocin Rush III:** Once the advice is implemented and success is seen, the helper or mentor can see they have been helpful and, again, this makes them feel good.

Not only does the mentor receive several rushes of feel-good emotions but also, when we provide advice, our world often becomes clearer. Providing advice on subjects we know and understand helps us to sort through our challenges.

Think about the adage, 'If you want to learn something, read about it. If you want to understand something, write about it. If you want to master something, teach it.'

Mentors spend time with people, both for the feel-good factor of giving back and because it allows them to sharpen their axe.

Don't be afraid of asking for regular contact with senior executives. The best ones know these benefits already and will be happy to help.

In the past, I have been disappointed when I have been asked for help and spent time mentoring but then heard nothing back. Silence is worrying – I am always looking for validation that the time spent was useful to the mentee. I don't mind if my suggestions aren't taken up, but it's important not to give advice in a vacuum.

This leads me to common excuses I hear when I finally catch up with mentees after a few months: 'I didn't have anything in particular to say,' or 'I hadn't taken any action from our conversation, so I didn't think I'd bother you.' There is *invariably* something to discuss, even if it's only 'No progress? Why not? What happened?'

Feedback is a vital part of the contract of mentoring – it's how a mentor knows whether they are helping and that the conversation was worth everyone's time. The feedback loop is there as much for your mentors as for yourself.

The consequence of not providing feedback to your mentor is that the next time you call, they will be less likely to help, feeling that the last conversation was a waste of time. You must therefore ensure you maintain regular contact with your Personal Board.

There is a fine line, though. If you have the best and brightest list of advisors, many of these people will be senior to you and at the top of their game, and they are unlikely to be constantly available at short notice for meetings. You need to strike the balance between a good level of regular contact and too much communication or too many meetings.

Keep in regular contact to maintain momentum and retain board members. Keep your Personal Board in the loop, especially after you have contacted them for advice.

These people will want to help. Experienced mentors, coaches and sponsors all understand that by giving back, by helping others in some way, they can also benefit. However, for them to feel this benefit, they need to understand that the time they have spent with you was valuable – valuable to *you* – and they need to see evidence of that.

Evidence of that value can come from all the uses of the Personal Board, for example:

- If a member has connected you with somebody useful, and the benefits you've experienced from that connection

- If your Personal Board has prompted you to deal with a challenge, what the outcome has been

- How you have been helped with a promotion or pay rise

Your board members will appreciate knowing that you have enacted the recommendations from your last session and set them in motion, resulting in forward progress. The rush of oxytocin will kick in, and they will be looking forward to the next opportunity to engage and to help.

MY STORY: A silent vacuum

Temper your ambition with reality

I have engaged with several people over the years who have asked me for help. I have spent time helping them to plot new journeys, promotions, business ideas, funding rounds, etc.

Most people naturally provide feedback on the sessions, talking about what was useful, confirming the actions they took from the meeting and sharing their progress.

However, some do not. In that vacuum, my curiosity always gets the better of me. I always want to understand whether the session was useful, what happened when the actions were taken and what they will be doing next.

I once spent two hours with a mentee I had worked with in a previous organisation, who had asked for my help on a promotion at another organisation. We concluded the session with three key actions and the mentee went on their way.

Weeks passed and I heard nothing.

Eventually, I reached out via LinkedIn to ask how they had got on. A short message of thanks and an update arrived in my inbox:

> Hi Emma,
>
> Thanks again for the time you spent helping me plan the next move.
>
> Following our meeting, I decided not to go for the role. However, I am looking at something else now and would love your view on how I could be successful. Do you have time tomorrow to catch up?

This message immediately deflated my mood. I couldn't help but feel the time we had spent together had not been valuable. I wasn't disappointed they hadn't gone for the role per se, but I was bothered that, after such a mammoth planning session, there had been no outcome. I was even more disgruntled that I needed to ask for the update.

If the mentee had reached out and said, 'Thanks for the time – super-valuable, but I realised I just wasn't ready and I'm now taking a different approach,' I wouldn't have minded.

In the real-life situation, though, I didn't prioritise a follow-up session. I waited until he chased a couple of times before I invested again. When I did, I was careful about the time I spent.

Feedback is important for your Personal Board members. Take the time to ensure they understand the value you have gained from the session, even if it's a change of strategy.

PRACTICAL TIP: Relevant actions

There are times when I have met with my Personal Board members and, even though I have provided all the background information and we have followed an agenda, brainstormed to the nth degree and taken subsequent actions, the situation has changed shortly after the meeting, through nobody's fault.

It is not uncommon for the business landscape to change quickly. As a result, the actions you have taken will, in hindsight, no longer be appropriate or relevant.

For example, perhaps you are planning a conversation about a pay rise. You meticulously plan with your Personal Board members the type of conversation you will have with your boss, how to approach the dialogue and what to ask for. Then your boss suddenly announces an automatic pay rise, making your planned conversations and actions redundant.

That's OK. Things change.

If you, for example, decide to back out of a conversation because of new information or decide not to go for a promotion, that's OK. However, I would always encourage you to keep your Personal Board members informed, so they are not left in a vacuum waiting for you to update them.

Remember: Your actions and progress are validation that the time spent was useful. Without action or progress, no value is realised, and the Personal Board member will likely feel cheated.

Sustaining your Personal Board

To ensure you keep the best and brightest engaged in your Personal Board, I would like to share the template that I use for my own Personal Board members.

This involves four simple steps:

1. **Share:** Define the goals for your engagement.

2. **Engage:** Meet with your Personal Board members.

3. **Act:** Take actions and deliver against them.

4. **Provide feedback:** Report on value and progress.

I have already covered all these steps, which represent the basics of any engagement regarding your goals. This quick template will therefore ensure that you continue to invest in and nurture your Personal Board.

1. Share: Define the goals for your engagement

Explaining why you need to engage with someone is the cornerstone of working with any mentor, sponsor or coach, or any other board member.

It's vital when you ask for *any time* with *anyone* for mentoring or career development purposes, that you clearly define what you hope to get out of the engagement.

Top tips

- Set goals for the meeting.
    - Use the scenarios in Chapter 8 to provide ideas.
- Be conscious of time.
    - How much time do you need?
    - How often do you need to meet?
- Set an agenda and provide background.
    - Be clear on what you are asking for and the likely outcomes.

Providing clarity on your needs and time will ensure that everyone knows what is expected from the engagement and what 'good' looks like as an outcome.

2. Engage: Meet with your Personal Board members

In your meeting, be enthusiastic, engaging and transparent, and use your time wisely regarding the desired outcomes. Think about how you can make this an enjoyable experience for your Personal Board members. Ensure that you remain conscious of time, again thinking about the value you want to get from the meeting.

Top tips

- Set an agenda and provide background before the meeting.
- Re-establish the agenda at the beginning of the session.
- Be conscious of time.
    - Focus on the agenda, avoiding unproductive conversations.
        - Keep checking the conversation is on track.
        - Try to avoid emotional stories.
        - Focus on only three actions/takeaways.

- In the end, recap on learnings from the session, your actions and takeaways, and other agenda items.

- Add some estimated timelines, especially for how and when you will provide feedback.

PRACTICAL TIP: How often to meet

How often you meet your Personal Board members will depend on your needs and the campaign you are running.

For example, if you are going for a new job or promotion, you will likely need several meetings in quick succession. However, if you are working on a long-term promotion, over twelve months, then monthly check-ins might be enough.

The important thing to remember here is to make sure everybody is aware of the expectations. When you set a meeting or agree on an action for the next meeting, ensure you have a conversation about when you might need to meet again.

Check this is acceptable to the Personal Board member. Do they have the time? Do they agree with the need and the agenda? Don't assume they can be at your beck and call.

Remember: Your actions and progress are validation that the time continues to be useful. This will help to sell the continued engagement.

---

3. Act: Take action and deliver

You've met with your Personal Board member, you've had a great session, and now you've gone back into the wild to start working on your new actions.

Remember that they are your actions to take. Now you need to prioritise so you can deliver on these actions.

Top tips

- Review your actions regularly – most likely weekly.
  - Consider any new information – are the actions still valid?
  - Assess your progress on the actions.
- Consider when you need to follow up with your Personal Board members.
  - What changes will need to happen and by when?
  - Book the next session (if you haven't already).

4. Provide feedback: Report on value and progress

Finally, as discussed at the start of this chapter, make sure you follow up with your Personal Board members. They will be eagerly awaiting feedback on your progress. Remember: It's up to you to provide feedback, not for your Personal Board member to have to chase you.

It's worth recognising that everyone has their preferences on how they receive feedback and progress updates, and you need to be cognisant of people's availability and time commitments. At the bare minimum, I strongly recommend you send a monthly email, LinkedIn message or text with feedback to update them on your progress.

When dealing with very senior executives who may sit on your Personal Board on fast moving subjects – like promotions or pay rises – it's important to understand how best to communicate or feed back to them quickly. Often, these executives cannot just be around for a quick catch-up after your latest interview in a series, for example. However, it's important that they hear the feedback to keep the oxytocin flowing. Ensure you check in on the best way to keep them updated as you execute your plan.

Top tips

- Provide feedback in real time and regularly.

  - Recap on the actions you took.

  - Outline your progress.

- Describe how you feel about the progress.
  - It's important to communicate that the action is delivering for you.
- Arrange the next check-in.
  - Let your Personal Board member know when they will hear from you again.

Being predictable as a mentee will ensure Personal Board members stay around and remain invested in your situation. Over time, as your goals change and your career evolves, you may choose to change your Personal Board members and the frequency with which you deal with them. However, you ideally want this to be your choice, so one of your feedback goals is retention.

Chapter review

Feedback is vital in nurturing your relationships with your Personal Board members.

The feedback loop you put in place is vital, both for your continued benefit and for the benefit of your Personal Board members. It is frustrating to invest your time and expertise in somebody and receive nothing back in return. A lack of feedback will quickly make any Personal Board dysfunctional.

Key takeaways

- Keeping your board up to date, engaged and ready to help is crucial to your success.

- Any mentor or coach needs to understand that the time they have spent with you was valuable and to see evidence of how they have helped you.

EXERCISE: Sustaining your Personal Board

Imagine how your feedback loop process might work in practice. It may differ for each Personal Board member, depending on your relationship and their seniority.

Make notes now on how you will apply the four steps of sustaining your Personal Board:

- **Share:** Think now about how you can define and articulate your goals.
- **Engage:** When, where and how will you meet?
- **Act:** Consider any potential actions from your first meeting.
- **Feedback:** How will you provide feedback and how often?

11
Board Assembled – Here's To Progress

These days, it's not uncommon to have four to six careers in a lifetime. Whether you climb a single ladder throughout your career or experience a wide variety of roles, with twists and turns and sideways steps, your network can shortcut nearly every step to help you progress faster.

To be clear: By 'shortcut', I am not suggesting that you might be cheating the process. Shortcuts are simply about finding better and more efficient ways to define and achieve the next steps in your career.

There is no doubt that by systematically working your networks rather than purely organically, you will be more laser-focused in your approach and make faster progress.

Having read this book, you should now know:

- How a Personal Board can help with your ambitions and dreams

- How to consider your goals and enlist the help of a Personal Board

- How to identify key people to make accelerated progress

- How to work with your Personal Board members, including key agendas and ways to ask for help

- How to keep Personal Board members close and sustain those relationships

Remember that building a Personal Board is about purposefully seeking out those who can help you the most. An organic collection of people will only get you so far, and Personal Board members should be there for your gain, not their own. That gives the biggest takeaway for anyone reading this book. Review your board regularly and ensure it's the best it can be, so you can be the best you can be.

I hope you are now excited about the prospect of starting to work with your Personal Board to achieve your goals. I am sure you will find many of your great ways for working with your Personal Board and, now you are thinking strategically about who you can work with, your board will go from strength to strength.

A final thought – I would love your feedback

Throughout this book, I've shared many of my own stories and stories of people who have adopted the idea of a Personal Board. If you have a story, I would love to hear it, so I can learn from it. I will also share it with others to inspire them, just as other people's stories have inspired you.

Please do reach out – I'd love to hear from you.

References

DISC personality testing, https://discpersonalitytesting.com, accessed 8 January 2023

Edgar, A, *Secrets of Successful Sales* (Panoma Press, 2018)

Edunov, S, et al, 'Three and a half degrees of separation', Facebook (February 2016), https://research.facebook.com/blog/2016/2/three-and-a-half-degrees-of-separation, accessed 8 January 2023

Fowler, B, 'The exact history of "Six Degrees of Kevin Bacon"', *New Zealand Herald* (31 August 2019), www.nzherald.co.nz/entertainment/the-exact-history-of-six-degrees-of-kevin-bacon/NCVVAU73UZ4TNCZAK726ENOBBQ/, accessed 2 February 2023

Harris, C, *Expect to Win: 10 proven strategies for thriving in the workplace* (Hachette UK, 2022)

Harris, C, *Strategize to Win: The new way to start out, step up, or start over in your career* (Hachette UK, 2022)

Kline, N, *Time to Think: Listening to ignite the human mind* (Octopus Publishing Group, 2021)

McKinsey & Company, 'Diversity wins: How inclusion matters' (May 2020), www.mckinsey.com/featured-insights/diversity-and-inclusion/diversity-wins-how-inclusion-matters, accessed 7 January 2023

Reed, J, *Why You? 101 interview questions you'll never fear again* (Portfolio Penguin, 2017)

Rosenberg McKay, D, 'How often do people change careers?' (The balance, 2020), www.thebalancemoney.com/how-often-do-people-change-careers-3969407, accessed January 2023

Tracy, B, *Eat That Frog!: 21 great ways to stop procrastinating and get more done in less time* (Berrett-Koehler Publishers, 2017)

Karinthy, F, *Everything is Different* (no publisher, 1929)

Lewis, AR, 'Teams solve problems faster when they're more cognitively diverse', *Harvard Business Review*, 7 (2017)

Reed.co.uk, 'Common interview questions and answers', www.reed.co.uk/career-advice/common-interview-questions-and-answers, accessed 9 January 2023

Summers, A, *One Train Later: A memoir* (Piaktus Books Ltd, 2006)

The Myers Briggs Foundation, www.myersbriggs.org, accessed 8 January 2023

Yong, E, 'The real wisdom of the crowds', *National Geographic* (31 January 213), www.nationalgeographic.com/science/article/the-real-wisdom-of-the-crowds, accessed 2 February 2023

Acknowledgements

Having been humbled by the generosity of so many people on my journey, this opportunity to say a little thanks, in print, is a huge honour.

My career took flight when I was nineteen years old and working for Ingram Micro. I met Andy Ogle from IBM. Andy saw the potential in me, and this led to an introduction to an IBM reseller, Oakbrook. Andy – the founding member of my original Personal Board – connected me to Dave Shepherd, Andy Weir, Dean Boyle, Kathy McKellar and the Oakbrook family. This family shaped me as a young professional and provided me with an opportunity to flourish in my career. Their kindness, integrity and generosity became the benchmark for all employers thereafter, setting a truly high bar.

I make an understatement in saying Andy made 'an introduction' to Oakbrook. Andy made the introduction, advocated for me, and coached me all the way through to success.

The idea that a person established in their career – Andy Ogle in this case – would have such faith in a nineteen-year-old, that they would expose their network for no personal gain, provided me with the determination to open my network to anyone who might need it in the future. This was the beginning of the Personal Board idea and 20+ years of finding opportunities for others in my network.

From Oakbrook, via a slight detour, I landed at Sun Microsystems. Another forever-family. Laura Turner joined my Personal Board as a mentor, then a peer and then she worked for me as I climbed the corporate ladder. A stalwart of the IT industry, a professional peer, a Personal Board member and lifelong friend, Laura gave me down-to-earth counsel and friendship, which is something I will never take for granted.

At Sun, looking for a change, I came across another other super connector in Brad Luton. Feeling my days at Sun were coming to an end, I looked for another role. While my profile didn't fit the criteria BMC were hiring against at the time, Brad advocated for me, and after an introduction to Donn D'Arcy, this connection triggered a seven-year journey into a world of fast-paced enterprise sales success and the beginning of my leadership journey. I wouldn't be where I am today without working with the team at BMC, for sure. For that I am eternally grateful.

As the years have progressed, other networkers have become central to new opportunities on the horizon – from new client relationships to investment opportunities. The perfect example is Nikki Watkins, a good friend, executive coach and one of the most focused human beings I know. She was introduced through Neil Greathead at BMC and, once I was connected to Nikki, her supportive, practical cheerleading provided me with a never-ending list of new connections I am thankful for. Nikki, like so many others, gives freely, knowing the universe has her back.

Through Nikki, I met Sarah Turner and Simon Hopkins, Founders of Angel Academe. Without a doubt, the team at Angel Academe and their group of 600+ angels are *the* most welcoming group of people I have ever met. Angel Academe's connections span the globe, with advice and support flowing freely to advisors and entrepreneurs. There I have been inspired by meeting Founders such as Laura Harnett, Lara Mott and Emma Sinclair MBE, to name just a few. In moving from a corporate career to a portfolio career, I found my tribe in Angel Academe, and their support has been unrelenting.

I'd also like to take a moment to thank my network for connecting me to those who helped create this book. Matt Wright, my partner in crime for the book, broke down this monster into bite-sized chunks to make the idea accessible to all. Tribeni Chougule would frequently remind me that she was waiting for her copy and always gave me a friendly reminder to 'get it done' – just the encouragement I needed. Also, my thanks go to Alison Edgar MBE for the introduction to Rethink, my publishers.

Finally, I am fortunate to have a backbone of support, which is unrelenting, in my friends and family.

My oldest friends – Emily, Jules and Jo – consistently ground me through any of life's curve balls. The pandemic brought us closer than ever. Always there for help, advice and fun to boot – every day.

And of course, thanks to Mum and Dad for their never-ending support. Providing a stable, supportive home to always come back to gave me my 'no fear of failure' attitude from a young age. I always knew I would have a roof over my head and good food on the table.

When people ask me who my coach is, Martin is my only answer these days. Martin has listened intently to every situation for over twenty-two years – counselling, coaching or simply providing a distraction as needed.

My career is Martin's accomplishment too, no doubt. Without Martin's support for me, our kids and our life together, my choices would have been different. I am forever grateful that Martin is Chair of the Personal Board.

Finally, I would like to thank everyone who has provided their stories for this book and who I have met on this journey. Inspired by your stories, I want to inspire more stories. You took the leap and found success, and now we get to celebrate that success in print. Forever. Congratulations.

The Author

Leaving school at sixteen, armed only with GCSEs, Emma's first job was as an administrator for Gossards in Leighton Buzzard. At the age of twenty, Emma found a passion for sales and customer success, in the process closing multi-million-dollar investment bank deals for the technology sector.

From there, Emma has worked her way up the ladder, job by job. She has led several businesses within the industry, working for technology companies such as Sun Microsystems, BMC Software and SAP.

Emma's financial success has allowed her to diversify into helping female-founded businesses with funding, having become an angel investor in 2018 through Angel Academe.

Attributing her career success to the network seeded in the early stages of her career and fostered throughout her last twenty-five years in business, Emma now works with start-ups, scale-ups and large enterprises, coaching their teams to higher growth.

🌐 www.emmamaslen.com

in linkedin.com/in/emmamaslen

📷 www.instagram.com/maslenemma

🐦 @emma_maslen